Christmas 1985

Merry Christmas Dad.
Love,
Anne + Tom

HUDSON'S HERITAGE

GRACE GOULDER IZANT

A CHRONICLE OF
THE FOUNDING AND THE FLOWERING
OF THE VILLAGE OF HUDSON, OHIO

THE KENT STATE UNIVERSITY PRESS 1985

Unless otherwise noted all photographs are from the collection of Grace Goulder Izant, the Western Reserve Academy Archives, and the Hudson Library and Historical Society.

Copyright ©1985 by the Kent State University Press, Kent, Ohio 44242
All rights reserved
Library of Congress Catalog Card Number 85-12714
ISBN 0-87338-323-0
Manufactured in the United States of America

Library of Congress Cataloging-in-Publication Data

Izant, Grace Goulder, d. 1984.
Hudson's heritage.

Bibliography: p.
Includes index.
1. Hudson (Ohio)—History. 2. Hudson (Ohio)—
Biography. 3. Hudson, David, 1761–1836 I. Title.
F499.H8I93 1985 977.1'36 85-12714
ISBN 0–87338–323–0

TABLE OF CONTENTS

PUBLISHER'S PREFACE

Grace Goulder Izant lived in the village of Hudson, Ohio, for six decades until her death in the fall of 1984 at the age of ninety-one. The present book, a history of the village, occupied her last years, though it had its genesis long before. Indeed, with this lady's boundless interest in local history, the book probably began on the day she moved to Hudson; her children recall growing up with the names of David Hudson, Birdsey Norton, Lemuel Porter, and others in this history as familiar to them as those of contemporary neighbors.

Granddaughter of a Great Lakes shipmaster, Captain Christopher Goulder, Mrs. Izant's roots were deep in the Western Reserve. After graduating from Vassar College in 1914, she went to work on the *Cleveland Plain Dealer* as society editor and women's feature writer. Robert J. Izant was movie editor on the paper, and when he went overseas as a lieutenant with the Thirty-seventh Army Division in World War I, she worked for the National Board of the YWCA in

New York and Europe, setting up rest centers for soldiers and war workers on leave. They married in 1919 and moved to Hudson in the fall of 1924, where she raised their family and he commuted to Cleveland where he was vice-president of Central National Bank.

Mrs. Izant's second writing career began in 1944 with an article about a trip to Columbus published in the *Plain Dealer* Sunday magazine. For the next twenty-five years her sketches of Ohio people and places were regular features of the magazine. They resulted in two collections, *This is Ohio* in 1953, revised in 1965, and *Ohio Scenes and Citizens* in 1964. *John D. Rockefeller: The Cleveland Years* was published in 1972.

A careful writer and meticulous historian, Grace Izant was not quite ready to release the manuscript to us before her death. There was always that final date to check, that last rounding out of a chapter. To the tribute she paid her daughter, Mary Izant White, in her acknowledgments we must add our own for the final gathering of the manuscript pages, the additional checking of facts from the various sources, and the general assumption of all those other least glamorous of an author's duties in meeting a publisher's fussy demands. We acknowledge as well those friends of Mrs. Izant who contributed much time and effort toward the design of this volume and the choice and preparation of the illustrations.

Grace Izant had not planned to carry the story beyond the death of James Ellsworth, but Mary White showed us the paper here included as an epilogue. This was a talk Mrs. Izant delivered to a local group in 1975, describing her arrival and early years in Hudson half a century before. This so well filled in the years between the end of her history and the present age, and so well conveyed the charm and voice of the author, that we couldn't resist including it to round out the book.

ACKNOWLEDGMENTS

This book owes much to many individuals and organizations. To name just a few of the latter: The Ohio State Historical Society, The Western Reserve Historical Society, the Cleveland Public Library, and, most importantly, the Hudson Library and Historical Society. Thomas Vince, Librarian, was unflagging in his enthusiasm and untiring in his assistance throughout the project. And James Caccamo, Archivist, deserves special mention for contributing to the historical notes and for indexing. The marvelous collection of Hudson history in their charge was an invaluable source.

Mrs. Eber Hyde, a direct descendant of David Hudson, patiently answered many questions and filled in many blanks, as did Anna Lee, David Hudson's great-great-granddaughter who lived for many years in the house he built, the first frame house in the village. Mrs. Morris Boyd, a lifelong resident of Hudson, also answered many questions and helped unravel several historical snarls.

Then there are those who provided encouragement, transportation, deed searching, and just every kind of support needed. To name a few: Betty Royon, Patricia Eldredge, Ellen Freemal, Priscilla Graham, Nan Herron, and Laura Cutshall, all of Hudson.

And I owe a very special debt of gratitude to two remarkable women without whom this never would have come into print: my daughter, Mary Izant White, and my dear friend Anne Hopkins Burnham. Their contributions made the difference. Their patience, perseverance, and "creative encouragement" enable me finally to say: FINIS.

Grace Goulder Izant
Great Elm, Hudson, Ohio
July 1984

DAVID HUDSON

. . . AS THE LAST BRITISH TROOPS WERE PUTTING OUT TO SEA . . .

TWO DAYS BEFORE Christmas 1783 David Hudson, a prosperous young farmer, and Anna Norton were married in Goshen, Connecticut, a small town in the northwestern section of the state. Anna was a cousin of David's friends, the Norton brothers, Birdsey and Nathaniel. The four, all in their early twenties, had grown up in Goshen, David coming as a small boy with his parents from his birthplace, Branford, in southern Connecticut. The bridegroom was the son of David Hudson senior, on several counts a man of mystery, but nonetheless a respected citizen and owner of a large and valuable farm. Anna was one of the numerous Norton clan, a prominent Goshen family.

Young Hudson and his bride, inured to Connecticut's austere Puritanism, would have shunned any show of nuptial finery or fanfare at their wedding. David probably appeared in his typical drab Sabbath day outfit, a skirted coat and leather smallclothes, his hair in a simple queue. Quite likely Anna wore homespun, suitable

attire for Connecticut's winter weather. It was especially welcome
garb if the ceremony took place in the plain little Congregational
Meeting House built the previous year on the green, and, according
to the stern orthodoxy of the period, never heated.

A new chapter was beginning for the young couple. And a new
era for America. The long war was over. On September 3 the peace
treaty had been signed in Paris. Dispatched across the Atlantic,
coming as fast as wind and sail could bring it, the document reached
New England shores the latter part of November.

In the meantime on the day of the Hudson-Norton wedding in
wintry Connecticut, General George Washington was making a
dramatic appearance before Congress, then sitting far to the south
in Annapolis. The general had come to the Maryland town from New
York City, where on December 4, as the last British troops were
putting out to sea and agitated Tories gathered on the dock for
passage to England or Canada, Washington had held an emotional
farewell meeting with his officers at Fraunces Tavern. After the last
tearful handshake, Washington left immediately for the South.
Stopping off in Philadelphia only long enough for final settlement
of his army accounts (he had accepted no pay as commander-in-chief),
he pushed on. Every mile of his progress became a triumphal
procession with people turning out all along the route to hail the
hero of the Revolution.

In Annapolis on the appointed day he found Congress assembled
with every seat in the big hall occupied and an overflow crowd of
admirers in the aisles. Washington took his stand before them, tall
and straight, every inch the commanding general. Resplendent in
his famous blue uniform and full military regalia, his sword at his
side, he addressed a tensely attentive Congress—and made world
history with every word and gesture. As he summed up his brief

speech he declared: "Having finished the work assigned me, I retire from the great theater of action, and bidding farewell to this August Body under whose orders I have so long acted, I offer my commission, and take my leave of all employments of public life."

Washington's audience, a colorful gathering in bright-hued silks and satins, powdered wigs and laces, listened profoundly moved by the significance of his message and of his presence among them. He, no less affected, bowed himself out as quickly as protocol would permit and soon was galloping off to Mount Vernon. He would be just in time for the Christmas Eve festivities he knew Martha was preparing for his homecoming.

David Hudson and his bride could look forward to no such holiday gaiety. In Calvinistic Goshen, Christmas Eve and Christmas Day would be no different from other days on the calendar—for the young couple the same farm chores, early and late.

David and Anna, however, were not to spend their lives on a Goshen farm. Before many years had passed, David with Birdsey Norton, soon joined by Nathaniel, would take title to thousands of acres in the distant Western Reserve—New Connecticut. In that uncharted frontier David would carve out a town that would be called Hudson, for him. Later another town nearby would be established named Norton for Birdsey who originally owned the land. Neither Norton brother, however, traveled west. But David did, and Anna and the children as well, and they made their home there. David would manage his own and the Nortons' share in the town called Hudson.

But in 1783 such a future was not even imaginable to the bride and groom who were starting married life on the big farm of David's father. On David senior's arrival in Goshen in 1764, when his son David was a small boy, he had purchased choice and extensive

farmland. Beside a scenic little lake then called Naushapaug Pond
he had built a three-storied "dwelling place" for his young family.
Villagers referred to the house deferentially as "The Hudson House"
and called it "a Mansion."

And well they might. Photographs taken in 1934 show it situated
on a rise with a bucolic view of the lake and the pasture beyond.
Later owners added a front porch the better to enjoy the outlook,
but even if one disregards the porch, the pictures tell a story of a
well-designed, commodious house where young David grew up and
where he took his bride. If Anna followed an old local bridal custom,
after the ceremony she traveled in the wintry December weather
to her new home on horseback, pillion style, behind one of her
husband's groomsmen.

The parental roof seems to have afforded adequate shelter for the
young couple and their rapidly increasing family for, according to
Goshen church records, they remained there until they left for the

Reserve in 1800. Shortly before their departure David senior died and his son David inherited the bulk of his estate, assets that help explain how a Goshen farmer could become an extensive landowner in the Western Reserve.

David Hudson, the son, was one of those individuals surfacing occasionally in history who seems born for his epoch. At thirty-nine when he traveled to the Reserve, David was older than most who braved the unknown frontier, but he was sturdy in body and mind and from the first made a success of pioneering. Undaunted by unbelievable hazards, instinctively a leader, he brought forth an enduring town where before his coming all had been virgin forest and unmapped wilderness. He fashioned it after villages in his homeland and, never hampered by self-doubt, ruled it as its undisputed head. He prospered, and with him his town prospered, soon outdistancing other neighboring pioneering efforts in the Western Reserve.

Born before the Revolutionary War, he knew from earliest childhood the increasing tensions between colonies and king. As a teen-ager he lived through the difficult, seemingly endless years of struggle. At twenty he heard the news of Yorktown that was soon to make him a citizen of the new United States. His life, spanning the administrations of the young country's first six presidents, reached well into the second term of the seventh, Andrew Jackson, the "first Democrat," and a man heartily opposed by Hudson, a loyal Federalist.

Hudson, Ohio, now approaching its twenty-first century, and benefiting from the advances the years have brought, at the same time retains an air of the early Connecticut village that Hudson founded. Numerous buildings and houses of his time survive, including his home, built in 1806. The campus of the college he founded, now Western Reserve Academy, is intact, dominated by the classic chapel completed in 1836, the year David Hudson died. The town is fortunate in its other numerous early nineteenth-century structures such as its fine old houses, all well cared for, and set amidst broad lawns and tall trees.

An appreciative and alert citizenry, guarding against the haphazard development that marks some neighboring towns, is dedicated to preserving Hudson's historic heritage and distinguishing charm. Gaining the attention of the federal government, Hudson has been listed in the National Register of Historic Places, and its main section designated as a Historic District.

The chronicle of David Hudson and his town enfolds also the story of the Western Reserve, those nearly three million virgin acres that soon became the starting area for young America's industrial heartland, and the gateway to the unexplored frontier of the new Far West.

Portrait by Ralph Earl courtesy of the Yale University Art Gallery.
ROGER SHERMAN

THE FATHER OF THE
WESTERN RESERVE

IN JANUARY 1784, less than a month after the Hudsons' wedding and Washington's "retirement," the Continental Congress ratified the final draft of the peace treaty. As one of the terms, Great Britain ceded to the new United States a vast western empire. To be known as the Northwest Territory, it was a frontier greater in area than that of any contemporary country save Russia. Out of this "Old Northwest" were to come the states of Ohio, Indiana, Illinois, Michigan, Wisconsin, and part of Minnesota. At the time no one in the Republic or in Great Britain had any conception of the territory's size or potential. Indeed, some leading Americans considered it a doubtful asset.

In that no man's land, David and Anna were to spend a great part of their lives, but in 1784, engrossed in their homemaking and the family farm, they doubtless gave little attention to treaty details as the news trickled into Goshen. Every Connecticut citizen, nonetheless, knew that through a concession by King Charles II, Connecticut for more than a hundred years had owned a piece of that frontier. It was a strip the width of the colony, stretching across

the continent all the way to the "South Seas." Further, the Royal Charter with a great seal affixed had made Connecticut an independent colony. At the time, speculation in western lands was rampant throughout the colonies. High-placed Americans, among them some of the founding fathers including Washington and Franklin, had acquired great tracts of British America.

The speculative land fever, temporarily checked by the war, broke out with new vigor once hostilities were over. David Hudson was beginning to enlarge his farm and was not yet looking westward. Connecticut, however, was not forgetting its stake in the new territory. Quickly joining the other states with colonial grants, it pressed Congress for these "rights." The landless states were heard from, too. Transappalachia, they contended, was a prize of the war which they all had supported, and now with victory were entitled to their share of the spoils.

The Continental Congress, confronted with many problems in this sprawling little-known demesne, was looking to its orderly administration, and particularly to sale of its lands for the benefit of a treasury bankrupt by the war. The lawmakers consequently ordered the land-claimant states to surrender their holdings to the federal government. Long and bitter opposition ensued, sharpened by disputes over boundary lines and overlapping grants; the royal cartographers in faraway London had had only the vaguest notion of American geography.

Finally Virginia, with by far the largest claims, yielded, settling for a section in the south-central Ohio country as bounty land for its unpaid Revolutionary War veterans. The other states followed Virginia's lead—all except Connecticut. The Nutmeg State alone refused to relinquish what it had had from the king. It was recalling, too, the Charter Oak of colonial days: how its plucky people had defied a titled English governor's order to surrender their Royal Charter. Hiding it instead in a giant oak tree, forever after called the Charter Oak, they had outsmarted the British and kept their independence.

This time Connecticut was holding out not alone for its Crown grant of 1662, but also because of an unresolved later issue: restitution for the catastrophe that during the war had engulfed its Wyoming settlements in Pennsylvania's beautiful Susquehanna Valley.

These colonies, established years before the Revolution (in the vicinity of present-day Wilkes-Barre), were well within Connecticut's allotment from King Charles. But it was found that the generous monarch later had allocated much of the same land to the Quaker William Penn. The flourishing little villages, maintained as Greater-Connecticut outposts, administered under Connecticut law and Connecticut jurisdiction, were resented bitterly by Pennsylvanians.

Fanned by tensions of the war, the continuing disputes erupted in July 1778 in a frightful raid by Indians and renegade Tories, all but obliterating the communities. David Hudson and the Nortons, teen-agers at the time, would have heard the holocaust decried in every Goshen home and on every Goshen street corner. No Connecticut citizen ever forgot Wyoming.

Seeking compensation for its lost settlements, and indemnity for the surviving residents, stubborn little Connecticut stood firm. Finally, if not the whole of its Royal grant, it agreed to accept as a compromise a part of it. All the while it was supported by its veteran congressman, Roger Sherman. Connecticut could have had no more effective ally. Sherman, whose first work had been as a shoemaker, became one of the most honored and influential leaders of the new Republic. He had been selected with Jefferson, John Adams, Benjamin Franklin, and Robert Livingston, to draw up the Declaration of Independence, and was the only man to sign the three great American documents, the Articles of Confederation, the Declaration of Independence, and the Constitution. He served ten years in the Continental Congress, and, named to the Supreme Court of Connecticut, was reappointed nineteen times. Although retired at the time of the Connecticut controversy, he plied his wiles from the wings, and won.

The outcome, an adroit political compromise maneuvered by the astute Sherman, represented another triumph for him and a very profitable victory for Connecticut. So it was that in May 1786, a horseman courier hurried the word to Hartford from New York where Congress was then sitting: Connecticut could keep for its own use—"reserve"—what proved to be a sizeable portion of the allotment from King Charles. Best of all, it was in the coveted Ohio country.

Connecticut had acquired a vast expanse of virgin territory larger than the state itself. It was thought at the time to include three million acres, although some estimated it as four million acres. Beginning at the Pennsylvania line it extended 120 miles along the southern shore of Lake Erie. Not by accident its width of from 50 to 70 miles about equalled that of the original Crown grant and in size it was close to the Wyoming area. This was indeed a rich prize that the "Shoemaker Senator" had gained for Connecticut. It was referred to at first as New Connecticut, then as Connecticut's Western Reserve, and finally as the Western Reserve. But to Connecticut citizens it always was New Connecticut. And it was here that David Hudson settled.

Few present-day residents of the Western Reserve are aware of its Wyoming genesis. Yet in its decade it was a familiar story. In England the tragedy was the subject of a widely read poem, *Gertrude of Wyoming*, by the British author Thomas Campbell. This tale of a beautiful bride killed in the massacre later became something akin to a best seller when introduced in America by the popular Washington Irving. Campbell's description of an idyllic, tropical Susquehanna Valley so moved Coleridge and Southey that it is said the two and some of their poet friends considered for a time leaving England to live on the scenic river banks.

The practical Roger Sherman labored under no such romantic urge as he successfully championed Connecticut's Wyoming cause, and thereby in a real sense became the father of the Western Reserve.

He was a familiar figure in Goshen where his brother, the not-so-admired Reverend Josiah Sherman was the minister of the Goshen Congregational Church from 1782, the year before David and Anna's marriage, until 1789, when "the town voted that he lay down his ministry." His had been a stormy pastorate.

Goshen, Connecticut, from an old woodcut by John Warner Barber.

LAND FEVER AND THREE WIVES

AMERICA'S INTEREST in western lands, rekindled by Connecticut's acquisition of the Western Reserve, reached its apogee in 1787. In that memorable year the Continental Congress passed the Northwest Territory Ordinance, thus supplying the mechanism by which the young country was to administer the vast dominion received from Great Britain in the Treaty of Paris. The ordinance was the magna carta for the New West, guaranteeing civil rights to its future citizens, prohibiting slavery, and providing for an orderly disposal of its far-flung lands. And it was the starting gun for that phenomenon of postwar America, westward migration.

So intense was the interest in the new territory that even before the official signing of the legislation, a group of high-ranking

Massachusetts war veterans were negotiating to buy a large block of the lands, their choice the Muskingum Valley area of the Ohio country. After encountering long and frustrating delays by the lawmakers, the veterans adroitly turned their support to the Congress president, General Arthur St. Clair who was jockeying to become governor of the immense area. The subtle wirepulling worked; the general saw to it that Congress passed the ordinance, won his appointment, and the veterans got their land.

News of the purchase aroused anew the go-west fervor. The movement, steadily gathering force and followers, made special inroads in New England, not only in Massachusetts but especially among Connecticut's restless, migration-minded people already clamoring for like ventures in their own Western Reserve.

David Hudson and Birdsey Norton were soon to be caught up in the ballooning furor. Yet it would seem that a wilderness future would have little appeal for either young man, for both appeared to be putting down their roots in Goshen. Hudson, working with his father, had begun to enlarge his farm. He had obtained flowage rights for two mills to be built beside the little lake that touched his grounds. Woolgrowing was being encouraged and sheep grazed in his pastures along with dairy cows in demand for Goshen's developing cheese industry.

On his part, Birdsey had completed an apprentice clerkship with the wealthy Goshen storekeeper, Ephraim Starr (whose daughter Hannah, he soon would be courting). Norton was about to open his own store in partnership for a time with his cousin Elihu Lewis. It was the first step in a career that would make Birdsey the area's foremost merchant. His inventories soon would range from ox yokes, plows, and firkins of butter, to satin from China, silks from India, and Hysong teas and chinaware brought by clipper ship in the growing Orient trade that developed early in Connecticut. Birdsey later had a part interest in one of these vessels with Oliver Wolcott, Jr.

Staid and settled though Hudson and Norton appeared to be, they were descended from adventuresome, pioneering forefathers and from them had land fever in their blood. Birdsey's brother, Nathaniel, was attracted early to the new territory opening up in western New York State. There he developed a tract of many acres that within a few years was to become the outfitting headquarters for David Hudson's trips to the new town he and Birdsey were to acquire in the Western Reserve. Another of the family, Captain John Norton, cousin of the Norton brothers, and brother of Anna Hudson, after service in the war was lured to frontier lands in Vermont. Resuming his peacetime vocation as a potter, he established there the Bennington Pottery, said to be the first pottery in Vermont.

Ebenezer Norton, father of Birdsey and Nathaniel, patriarch of the Goshen Nortons and founder of their fortune, set the pattern for the family's pursuit of new lands. Coming to Goshen in 1739 when it was little more than a frontier outpost, Ebenezer took over lands his father, Samuel, had bought at auction at bargain prices. Ebenezer, young and enterprising, gave his energies to the town's development. When Hudson senior arrived with his family in 1764, Ebenezer was a prosperous, leading citizen. Like him, the elder Hudson had spent his young years pioneering in new territory, but at forty-five when he settled in Goshen, Hudson's days of roaming were over.

Hudson senior had come from Branford, an attractive town in southern Connecticut where he had lived for twelve years. His home prior to his arrival there is not known, but wherever it was, from some as yet undisclosed wellspring he had come into plenty of money. And with his move to Branford he was prepared to spend it.

Hudson is first mentioned in Branford in the town record in 1754, "when he did pay Moses Foote two thousand and one-hundred twenty-three pounds local money of the Colony for 17 acres and 15 rods on Sibbie Hill." The price is roughly equivalent to $10,000 in the 1980s. It was an incredibly large amount for the time, especially when money was scarce and barter was generally relied upon. Also the sum seems large for so small an acreage. But Sibbie Hill had much to offer: "a dwelling house," a barn and shop, a wall (probably of stone), and an orchard. To justify the price the appurtenances would have been very fine indeed. And maybe they were.

The deed was made out to "David Hudson, taylor," an unexplained designation. It is the only such reference to him that occurs, and remains one more unanswered detail about this enigmatic man. For the next ten years he continued to buy Branford real estate, in all acquiring an additional two hundred acres in small plots. He paid a total of "335 pounds lawful money" for these purchases, or about equal to $1,000 today.

The Sibbie Hill property was evidently in a desirable section of Branford as it adjoined that of Daniel Baldwin of the wealthy Baldwin family. Hudson was made a Freeman of the town, which conveyed a certain social prestige and gave him the right to vote. He was "now associating with the best people in town," he noted.

Soon he could "enjoy one half of a Sabbath Day House in partnership with my neighbor Baldwin," he wrote. These structures, often erected on village greens, and equipped with well-stoked stoves, were a welcome refuge to "outdwellers" coming into town in winter for the all-day Sunday assemblies in the meetinghouses that, according to stern Puritan doctrine, were never heated. Parishioners gathering before the well-fired stoves fortified themselves for the long morning sessions. At noon they returned to warm up again and to eat their midday meal brought from home and prepared Saturday.

In 1754, David Hudson senior was thirty-three, according to Connecticut genealogist Donald Linus Jacobus's reckoning, and in love. He had much to offer a wife, and lost no time in wooing his choice, Kezia Rose, daughter of a prominent local family. In April, a few months after Hudson acquired Sibbie Hill, the two were married. They shared a short interim of happiness, for Kezia died the following January, probably in childbirth. Her baby, named David, lived only until spring.

In August of the next year the widower traveled to Guilford, Connecticut where he married Rebecca Fowler. She was two years older than her bridegroom and the daughter of a successful shoemaker and tanner. The following September (1756) Rebecca gave birth to a girl. Her husband named the child Kezia for his first love. Three sons followed: Timothy in 1758; the Ohio David Hudson, February 17, 1761; and John in 1762. John may have died early as no further reference to him occurs.

Little is known about Rebecca. She was mentioned in 1769 in her father's will, indicating that she was living at that date and therefore would have accompanied the family on the move in 1764 to Goshen. She died sometime before 1777, since that year her father's will was probated and Rebecca's share went to her heirs. There are few references to this mother of the Ohio David Hudson. She probably was buried in Goshen, but if so her grave is not marked.

At some as yet undisclosed time and place Hudson made a third excursion into matrimony. The new wife appears merely as Sarah. Nothing further was recorded about her until her death. She had outlived her husband, and in a Goshen Town Hall record it was noted that "the Mrs. Hudson who died in January, 1805 of old age at 74 was the widow of David Hudson senior." Accordingly she had been ten years younger than her husband, a good age at which to act as surrogate mother to his children.

Sarah, then, was mistress of the Hudson House when it was home also to young David and Anna following their marriage. If, as local church records indicate, they lived there until leaving for the West, seven of their nine children (including a short-lived David who died in 1796) were born during their stay. There is no record of how Sarah coped with this burgeoning household.

Like Rebecca, Sarah probably is buried in a Goshen cemetery, her burial place also lacking identification. The beloved Kezia, on the other hand, lies in a North Branford cemetery, her baby David beside her, both interments clearly marked.

GENERAL ANTHONY WAYNE
Greenville Treaty Calumet

DAVID HUDSON'S
FIRST WESTERN
ACRES

I N EVERY GATHERING of Connecticut people the conversation
was certain to turn to the Western Reserve, New Connecticut
to them. They viewed it as an extension of their homeland, a
region rightly theirs. Land speculation was epidemic and the state's
delay in opening the territory roused loud denunciation. The elder
Hudson, growing old with Sarah amidst a bevy of grandchildren,
heard the talk. He scarcely could have avoided hearing it because
his son David, David's friends, and their Goshen neighbors seemingly
could think of little else than this alluring region. No one had much
information about the territory, but no matter, wishful thinking made
up for facts. A rosy glow enveloped the country across the
mountains. To householders, weary from the long war, to farmers

struggling with worn-out, rock-littered soils, and to speculators—especially to speculators—the region beckoned irresistibly. And the old man, listening to it all, anchored by the pile-up of his years, did he perhaps feel a nostalgic stirring of his youthful wanderlust?

Despite the mounting pressure to make the Reserve available to the people, the state assembly delayed doing so. The fact was, the distant, little-known area that Connecticut had fought so hard to win had become something of a white elephant to officials managing it in Hartford, and the decision was made to sell it. The Salt Springs Tract near the future city of Youngstown already had been sold. Another five hundred thousand acres in the northwest corner of the Reserve, known as the Fire Lands or the Sufferers' Lands, had been set aside to reimburse Connecticut citizens for losses in the war. What remained was an immense territory. Land company officials studying the crude maps then available were certain it covered three million acres even without the Fire Lands. Some thought it even larger. A committee of eight, one man from each Connecticut county, was appointed to take charge of the sale. The price was to be no less than one million dollars.

Two sales efforts were attempted. Both failed, due mainly to stepped-up hostilities by the Indians, especially the fierce Shawnees. There was apprehension, too, about the British, who contrary to postwar agreements remained in many garrison posts carrying on lucrative fur trading with the Indians and at the same time encouraging them in their anti-American incursions.

George Washington, elected president in 1789, had not forgotten the Ohio country where as a youthful scout for Governor Dinwiddie of Virginia he had his first military experiences. He lost no time in dispatching an expedition to the West with orders "to rid the area of the Indian menace." (The president shared his fellow citizens' notion that the new land was theirs to appropriate.) The first sortie led by General Jacob Harmar was routed by the tribesmen. A second attempt under General Arthur St. Clair, governor of the Northwest Territory, met an even more disastrous defeat. The jubilant Indians meanwhile stepped up their forays.

Washington then selected General Anthony Wayne for a third attempt. Unlike the previous two leaders, Wayne was supplied with adequate equipment, took time to train his men thoroughly, and understood Indian warfare. Living up to his wartime soubriquet, "Mad Anthony," in August 1794 he vanquished the tribes in the battle of Fallen Timbers near today's Ohio-Indiana line south of the future site of Toledo, and finished off his victory with systematic destruction of the Indians' cornfields and villages.

In the meantime everyday life went on in Goshen and, with little thought of Wayne's activities in the faraway wilderness, David Hudson senior in June 1794 sat down to make out his will. His "dear and well beloved wife Sarah" (regrettably no mention of her maiden name) was to have one-third of his real estate and his "household stuff" during her lifetime. The "remaining part of the lot at the mouth of Naushapaug Pond" was designated "for my son Timothy along with ten pounds lawful money which my son David is to pay to the said Timothy." His daughter Kezia Parmele (she had married Theodore Parmele of Goshen) was to receive "ten acres lying at the southeast corner of my home lot, leaving the head of the spring of water two rods to the north of it, and also my household stuff after my wife's decease. Finally, I give to my son David all the rest of my land wherever it may be with my wife's third portion after her decease, and also my dwelling house [the Hudson House where all the Hudsons were then living] and barn." The value of the estate is not known. But considering the elder Hudson's financial achievements, it can be assumed his son David as chief beneficiary was in line for a substantial legacy. His father named David and Theodore Parmele, his son-in-law, as executors. Thus David early was aware of the heritage he was to have.

Meanwhile Chief Justice John Jay on a trip abroad had obtained assurances from the British of their early removal from American territory. At the same time word had reached Hartford of Wayne's victory over the Indians. The Connecticut assembly in anticipation of the Greenville Treaty (they rightly assumed the tribes had no choice but to sign it) again made plans to offer New Connecticut for sale. This time the money realized was to be set aside as a permanent fund, with the interest allocated to support the state's public schools. Although the arrangement would amount for a time to a lien on the territory, it appealed to Connecticut's twin concerns for land and learning and helped promote the sale.

The sale of the Western Reserve had been advertised in all Connecticut newspapers and crowds of hopeful purchasers hurried to the Hartford Court House. One wonders if young David Hudson and Birdsey Norton, so soon to have major roles in the Reserve, were among the throngs.

With two sections already taken from the Reserve, officials decided against further piecemeal disposition of the new land. No one had any clear idea of the territory's exact size, but obviously it was very large, too much for an individual to finance. Nonetheless buyers' interest was intense. Sharply competing coalitions formed only to break up with rejection of each offer.

At length on September 2, 1795, a month after the signing of the Greenville Treaty, a syndicate of thirty-five men (the number later increased) taking the name the Connecticut Land Company offered $1,200,000 for the entire tract, and their proposition was accepted. Little cash changed hands. Money was scarce and deals were financed largely by personal notes or mortgages on the land at 6 percent. Interest payments earmarked for the school fund were not to start until two years after purchase.

Company officials had only vague information about their purchase, but the men figured they had paid forty cents an acre, possibly less. This was a purely speculative undertaking and at such a price a substantial profit on re-sale seemed assured. One group estimated it was a four-million-acre tract, and wildcat transactions ensued in a short-lived Excess Land Company.

The largest share ($116,118) in the Connecticut Land Company was held by Oliver Phelps, bellwether in organizing the company. Joining with Gideon Granger (to be postmaster general under President Jefferson), Phelps invested an additional $80,000. A compulsive speculator, Phelps, with Benjamin Gorham, already had taken title to vast lands in New York State in what became the Phelps-Gorham Tract. Phelps also bought into the ill-fated Excess Land Company. Over-extended, like many of his contemporaries, he spent his later years wrestling with bankruptcy, ultimately dying in debtor's prison. But if fortunes were lost, fortunes also were made.

The only company member from Goshen was Ephraim Starr, who held $17,415 worth of shares. With Starr one of the company, his son-in-law Birdsey Norton (he and Hannah had married three years before) and David Hudson would have had ready access to information not only about company land but on inside details of the entire project as well. With the canny Starr's reputation for never having made an unprofitable move, the two friends, so long interested in the New West, were impatient to participate in the venture.

The company, to get on with its business, deeded its lands in trust to three members: John Caldwell, Jonathan Brace, and John Morgan, all of Hartford. The trustees in turn "granted deeds to each company member for his share proportionate to his investment as measured in twelve hundred thousandths" of the still unsurveyed Reserve. A deed executed on September 5, 1795, three days after the land company purchase, certified that Ephraim Kirby and Elijah Wadsworth, both of Litchfield, "were entitled to twenty thousand twelve hundred thousandths of the Connecticut Western Reserve" (interpreted as one-sixtieth of the tract).

In the meantime company officials were working on details for a series of lotteries known as draughts, or drafts, by which the lands were to be offered to the public. Obstacles were encountered and the drafts had to be temporarily delayed. Waiting no longer for this procedure, Kirby and Wadsworth, like several other stockholders, "found it expedient" to sell sections of their holdings whenever they could find purchasers—in other words, they needed the money.

One such buyer was David Hudson. A deed made out to him October 10, 1795 in Hartford reveals that Kirby and Wadsworth "received $1500 from David Hudson, Jr. for 3000 acres in the Territory south of Lake Erie, called the Western Reserve provided said Territory is found to contain 3,000,000 acres." Hudson was to have what would be the equivalent of "one-thousandth part" (something less than 3,000 acres). Thus he paid about fifty cents per acre. It was further specified that this property "would lie within the proportion of the Western Reserve to which we are entitled."

Like Hudson, Birdsey Norton with Elihu Lewis as well as several officers of the land company, among them Moses Cleaveland, were quick to take advantage of the early purchase opportunities. Some bought much larger sections than Hudson. With speculation at fever pitch buyers encountered no difficulty in re-selling for quick profits.

No recognizable reference to this early purchase has been found in Hudson's papers, no hint of the deal itself. It appears for many reasons, however, to have been in what ultimately became Medina County. The men from whom Hudson bought his land, Kirby and Wadsworth, also acquired land in that section. One of the important towns in the future Medina County was named Wadsworth for Elijah Wadsworth although he never lived there. Numerous notations later in Hudson's journals as well as courthouse records refer to land transactions in what would be the Medina County area. In 1816, for example, Hudson sold a good-sized farm in Wadsworth township to his friend Frederick Brown, Owen Brown's brother, who became a leading citizen there. Adjoining Brown's property Hudson's son Timothy managed a farm that belonged to his father. Owen Brown's adopted son Levi Blakeslee, following his foster father's trade, operated a tannery near Wadsworth on land that he purchased from Hudson. The property that Hudson had bought sight unseen proved to be valuable, and its acquisition indicates he had ample resources, even if like most transactions of the day it was underwritten in part by a mortgage—at 6 percent.

The haste of Connecticut men to acquire Western land reflected the mood of the young country that was pushing out its boundaries, eagerly reaching into a new world. Even men's dress was changing. Powdered wigs and laces were disappearing, knee pants and silk stockings giving way to pantaloons, more serviceable for pioneering. The federal government, keeping abreast of the times, was preparing to move the capital from staid and settled Philadelphia to the new city-in-the-making called Washington. President Washington already had braved its mud, and in full Masonic dress had dedicated the cornerstone of the Capitol's first section. Construction also had begun on the White House, referred to as the President's House, sometimes as the President's Palace.

GENERAL MOSES CLEAVELAND
Portrait by Hudson artist Avis Andres.

Canterbury, Connecticut, from an old woodcut by John Warner Barber.

THE LAND COMPANY LEARNS
ABOUT ITS PURCHASE

PROBLEMS BESETTING the Connecticut Land Company were keeping its affairs at a standstill. Stockholders eager to begin selling what they had bought and would-be buyers pressed for action. But the tract would not be offered to the public because the necessary information about it was lacking. Even its size was as yet not determined, though it was apparent the four-million-acre figure was unrealistic. Little, however, had been learned of the Reserve's vast interior, its lakes, rivers, hills, and valleys.

Of the several early surveys even the most recent, completed in 1787 by United States Geographer Thomas Hutchins, had not been wholly satisfactory. One of the few early books on Ohio, Jedidiah Morse's *The American Geography*, published in 1789, touched only lightly on Connecticut's Reserve. The author warned of the area's poisonous snakes, spoke of the abundance of game and fish, and enumerated its varieties of trees (the sugar maple, he declared the most useful), but he failed to mention such important landmarks as the Cuyahoga River! Nonetheless, so great was the interest in the distant domain that the book, inadequate as it was, became a best seller. David Hudson acquired a copy and brought it with him when he came to the Ohio country.

A comprehensive investigation was called for, and in the spring of 1796 the land company sent out an exploratory and surveying expedition headed by Moses Cleaveland of Canterbury, Connecticut. A general in the state militia during the Revolutionary War, Yale graduate, and successful lawyer, Cleaveland was a company director, owning $32,600 worth of stock. Also he had participated in the early land buying. The general would have a personal interest in exploring the new land.

The outfit included fifty experienced surveyors, chainmen, axmen, boatmen, and general helpers, with cattle on the hoof and generous supplies of whisky and rum. Indian dress also was included for use by Cleaveland when he met with tribesmen, as well as plenty of trinkets for the "savages." The group faced all the hazards and dangers of an unknown country, endured pelting rain and summer heat, swarms of insects, illness, and some serious accidents.

At Buffalo Creek they were met by representatives of the powerful Six Nations. In accordance with land company policy to maintain friendly relations with the Indians, the general stayed there for three days entertaining the delegation with a feast and plenty of liquor. The swarthy-faced Cleaveland, donning his Indian regalia and looking like an Indian himself, listened to Indian demands and agreed to try to get officials to grant the representatives what they wanted. In return for Indian lands that the white man was about to take over, the tribesmen asked for a $300 annuity from Congress, or if that failed, $1,500 in cash. Cleaveland concluded the colloquy in a gesture of goodwill with the gift of two beef cattle and one hundred gallons of whisky. Farther along another group of Indians was placated with glass beads for the women and whisky for the braves.

Conneaut, the Plymouth of the Reserve, in July 1796.

Two weeks later, after tedious, discouraging progress through the wild, unfamiliar terrain, Cleaveland's party crossed the Pennsylvania line into the Western Reserve at what is now Conneaut. And it was the Fourth of July! A gunfire salute immediately was sounded to the first Independence Day in the state of New Connecticut. (The Reserve, it was generally understood, would become a new state with this name.) From their final organization at Dover in eastern New York State near the Connecticut border, the explorers had been forty-eight days on the way. Ready at last for a celebration, they

raised well-filled mugs in a series of toasts to one and sundry
beginning with President Washington. "After several pails of grog
were drunk they closed with three cheers, supped and retired in
remarkably good order," Cleaveland noted in his journal with a rare
touch of humor.

They tarried here only briefly. Cleaveland had instructions from
the land company to "establish a city" in the heart of the Western
Reserve, and he was eager to be on the way. He selected a site on
the shore of Lake Erie where the Cuyahoga River empties into the
lake, twisting and turning to create a fine harbor. He thought to
call the place Cuyahoga, but his men to honor him gave it his name.
One of his mapmakers lettered the name in as "Cleveland," a spelling
that eventually was adopted.

Three years after Cleaveland laid out his "city," David Hudson
would be beaching his boat on this shore en route also to found a
town.

For General Cleaveland it had been an arduous expedition. The
coming on of winter plus the men's numerous illnesses and overall
exhaustion cut short the work. The contingent headed for
Connecticut, leaving half the survey unfinished. On their return,
land company officials, especially the stockholders, were distraught.
They had spent $14,000 of company funds and still had no real idea
of the territory they had purchased.

New assessments were issued against the shareholders and another
surveying party sent out, arriving in the Reserve early in 1797.
Although better organized and equipped than the first, it also was
beset by accidents and sickness. Four men drowned, among them
the chief boatman, Captain Joseph Tinker, who lost his life in a
swollen stream that his companions named Tinker's Creek in his
memory. And so it has been known ever since as it wanders in

devious fashion in and out of today's Summit and Cuyahoga counties. Practically every man was affected by dysentery or malaria. The outfit apparently was supplied with the medicines of the day and journal entries note frequent resort to "a strong puke."

The second group discovered that early maps and calculations which had been relied upon were misleading. In one case, for example, 30,000 acres were found to lie under Lake Erie. When the work was completed and surveyor Augustus Porter's report submitted, the land company learned the Reserve contained 3,450,753 acres. The figure, questioned by the Excess Land Company, was checked by a Yale mathematics professor and found to be accurate. The Excess Land Company had nothing.

Porter's overall figure included the Fire Lands area, which he found had 496,590 acres. This left the land company with 2,954,163 acres to sell. While not as much as some had hoped for, it nonetheless was a magnificent dominion. From this main body of the Reserve, eight entire Ohio counties eventually were formed: Ashtabula, Geauga, Lake, Trumbull, Cuyahoga, Portage, Medina, and Lorain, as well as half of Mahoning and most of Summit where David Hudson was to locate.

Hartford, Connecticut, courtesy of the Western Reserve Historical Society.

THE GREAT REAL ESTATE LOTTERY

FOLLOWING THE TWO exploratory surveys the Connecticut Land Company marked off the Western Reserve in townships and ranges, checkerboard fashion. The range lines ran east and west beginning at the Pennsylvania border, crossing townships which were platted south to north. The company disposed of its land by these townships in a series of lotteries or draughts (drafts). In one of the first of these, January 1798, Hudson Township was sold.

Each township contained 16,000 acres, more or less. It was to measure five miles on each side and sell for $12,900, or close to that figure. Measurements often varied by a few acres because of the unreliability of early surveying instruments and difficult terrain.

The lotteries, which took place in Hartford, were repeated at various times in 1798, 1799, 1802, 1807, and 1809 until all the lands

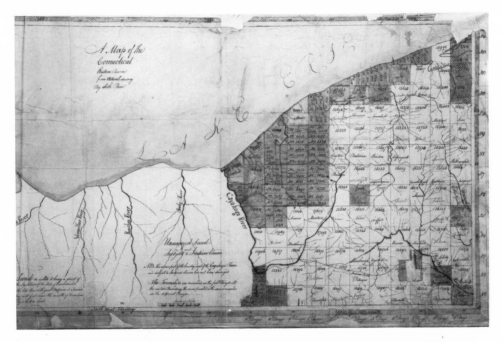

Map of the Connecticut Western Reserve, made by Seth Pease in 1798.

were sold. At that time the land company, which was unincorporated, was dissolved. Until 1802 only the Western Reserve lands east of the Cuyahoga River were entered in the lottery. Hudson Township fell within this section. After Indian claims were further negotiated, lands west of the river also were sold off. These townships, which were larger than those disposed of earlier, were higher priced.

An entire township was sold at each drawing. To meet the price a number of buyers usually pooled their resources. One of them then picked from a box a numbered certificate designating a specific township. The buyers could not select their township and, except for its designation on the land company maps, had little idea of its locale. Following the drawing the acreage was prorated according to each individual's investment.

Hudson Township—officially Township 4, Range 10—was drawn by David Hudson, Birdsey Norton, and thirteen others. They paid the company price, $12,903.23 and drew a township of 15,969 acres, only slightly less than the established size. David Hudson invested $900.00, Birdsey Norton with Elihu Lewis $300.00. Samuel Fowler, whose share was $1,546.77, did the drawing for the group. The largest single share was Ephraim Starr's $6,000.00; the smallest was the $.03 invested by Stephen W. Jones. The only woman of the group, Julianna Hubbard, paid in $200.00. After the drawing, as was the case generally with the lotteries, the fifteen disposed of their portions or added to them by exchanging parts of their acreage with each other or by buying and selling other sections. Such deals were consumated often by notes and mortgages with relatively little cash changing hands.

To compensate for hills, wet lowlands, or other undesirable sections of a township, the land company set aside "equalizing" areas. Because of swamps in the western part of Township 4, the company donated 6,007 acres in what is now Geauga County. It was "for the common good of all who had participated in Draft 59." Most of Township 4 had good land. The swamps in what is now the Mud Run area were of limited extent and when drained later became productive farmland. The equalizing grant, however, was accepted gladly. It brought the total land to 21,976 acres and reduced the overall per acre price from a little over eighty cents to about fifty-nine cents.

Although Nathaniel Norton is not listed as a participant in the lottery, he apparently was a silent partner with Birdsey (the two were seldom separated in any activity). The two Nortons, as is clear from subsequent events, owned all of Township 4 at the conclusion of the lottery except for Hudson's $900.00 share.

According to a legal agreement signed by the Nortons on January 29, 1800, Hudson borrowed $2,325.60 from them. The loan was to be repaid in full in a little over seven years, by which time it was specified the sum due would be $4,320.00, the original $2,325.60 plus $1,994.40 interest at 6 percent, the going rate for such loans. "It [the loan] is expressly designed," the document stated, "to convey to said David the proportion of $2,325.60, original purchase money of all lands and other property . . . belonging to Draught 59." In other words, the Nortons were enabling Hudson to acquire township land at the same price they had paid for it in the original draft.

The $2,325.60 plus Hudson's original $900.00 investment came to $3,225.60, or one-fourth of the original purchase price. Consequently he was entitled to one-fourth of the township's 15,969 acres, or nearly 4,000 acres. With his one-quarter share of the 6,007 equalizing acres, a trifle more than 1,500 acres, Hudson owned close to 5,500 acres. The Nortons and Hudson, the three friends so long interested in Connecticut's Western Reserve, became the "proprietors," or owners, of Township 4, Range 10. Designating themselves "The Company," they were in charge of the area's development. Officiating from Connecticut, Birdsey was the chief executive, as it were, but on-the-spot management of the township and its affairs would be wholly Hudson's province.

With land company records so specific and so readily available, it is hard to understand the frequently repeated statement that the township was purchased for $8,320 and that because "it was largely swamps" a compensating 10,000 acres were donated by the Connecticut Land Company. This supposedly reduced the per acre price to thirty-two cents—a deal the company officials certainly would have found hard to accept.

Such accounts also claim the township was drawn by six men,

Hudson and the two Nortons plus Benjamin Oviatt, Stephen Baldwin, and Theodore Parmele. A plaque over the door of the Hudson Library and Historical Society honors the six as the "Founders of Hudson." But plaque or not the names of Oviatt, Baldwin, and Parmele do not appear in local annals until April 1800, when as a group they bought one-eighth share of the township. The deed to the three men was drawn up by Birdsey Norton. It specified that "in consideration of 1612.90, being one-eighth part of original purchase money for Draught 59" one-eighth part of the township is transferred to Oviatt, Baldwin, and Parmele "as tenants in common with Nathaniel Norton, David Hudson and myself." Again Birdsey was giving the three men the land at the figure it had cost him. This was all two years after Draft 59 was run, and one year after David Hudson had established the village.

These new investors were citizens of Goshen, neighbors of Hudson and the Nortons. Doubtless they had listened to the Nortons' and Hudson's enthusiastic descriptions of New Connecticut and had decided to risk a conservative investment in it. All were connected by blood or marriage: Parmele was married to Hudson's sister, Kezia, Birdsey's and Nathaniel's mother was a Baldwin, and Oviatt's son Luman had married a Norton.

None of the original Oviatt-Baldwin-Parmele group made the trip to Ohio, but as Summit County records attest, they carried on from Goshen a lively and complicated speculation in Ohio land transactions. They sent their sons and daughters to Hudson, numbers of them. Apparently not interested in parental land in the Geauga County equalizing tract, the younger generation settled in Hudson. Before long the village was plentifully peopled with young Oviatts, Baldwins, and Parmeles from whom many present-day inhabitants are descended.

David Hudson invested in absentia in many subsequent drafts. This was true of Birdsey, too, probably handling Nathaniel's money with his own, and also of Ephraim Starr. The latter's investments were often in the $6,000 range while Birdsey in at least one case invested $10,000. Hudson's initial share in every draft was $900. He soon held title to plats in such widely scattered localities as Cleveland, Perrysville, Euclid, Mentor, Painesville, Newburgh, Youngstown, Warren, and other parts of the Reserve, not to overlook his purchase in 1795 of those 3,000 acres in the then uncharted New Connecticut. Before long he controlled many hundreds of acres and constantly was occupied with disposing of some and acquiring others. In the absence of specific records, there is no way of knowing the size at any one time of his holdings.

He gave a great deal of attention to his share of the equalizing acres in Geauga County and his name appears repeatedly in transactions of this land. Evidently he added substantially to his original share; he had enough acreage by 1812 to sell Nathaniel Norton twenty separate pieces that came to 2,960 acres, almost half of the original equalizing grant.

He apparently thought highly of his Geauga County property, retaining some of it all his life, allotting and selling other sections for home sites. He donated six and a half acres in 1811 "as an expression of good will for the inhabitants of Wooster Township [now called Chester, Wooster Township was originally named for the Revolutionary War hero, General David Wooster] to be used forever as a public park." Today this is a plot of well-cared-for gardens and lawn, shaded by tall trees. Laid out as a square, it lies at the junction of two old highways, Mayfield Road (Route 322) and Chillicothe Road (Route 306). A huge conspicuously placed boulder memoralizes David Hudson as the donor.

THE HOWLING WILDERNESS

IN 1798, not long after David Hudson and the Nortons had acquired their New Connecticut township, the senior Hudson died. On May 3 of that year Sarah Hudson signed a quitclaim deed relinquishing to David Hudson, her stepson, her right as stipulated by her husband's will to his real estate, land, and buildings as well as her dower rights. This was "in consideration for two hundred pounds received to my satisfaction of David Hudson." When distribution of the will took place the following year, it was noted that "the widow of the deceased has given a quitclaim of all her right and title to said estate for the security of fifteen pounds to be paid her annually by David Hudson." Whether this was in addition to the two hundred pounds of the previous agreement, or instead of it, is not clear. It appeared, however, that Sarah was not to have any of her husband's property. Nothing more is heard of her until six years later when her death is recorded in Goshen.

The will's other provisions were carried out: David's sister, Kezia, received her lot of land and cash allocation; his brother Timothy's share was assigned to his heirs since he had died recently. As the old man had indicated, the rest of his land (now including the wife's third portion), the house, and barn were turned over to his son David. This inheritance plus the six hundred acres the younger David owned in Goshen made him indeed a man of substance.

It was a busy time for him. Distribution of his father's will took place on April 13, 1799, and nine days later he was to leave for the West to take possession of the township in the Reserve.

Like many of his contemporaries, David Hudson had been "contaminated," as he put it, by the publications of Thomas Paine, Hume, and other philosophers of the French Revolution. On the eve of his departure for the Reserve, he was persuaded to attend one of the revival meetings prevalent in that area. This was at the local church, conducted by the new minister, the popular Reverend Asahel Hooker. Writing a few years later in a missionary magazine, Hudson described how he was moved in spite of himself by the exhortations of Hooker. Under the eloquence of the minister he "confessed his infidelities and blasphemies against Jesus Christ and the Gospels and was vouchsafed salvation." (In his article Hudson stated the date of the meeting was 1798, but according to church records it took place in 1799.)

In this sudden turnabout from earlier anti-Christian diatribes, David felt self-conscious and embarrassed to face his friends and neighbors. Consequently "I decided," he wrote, "to remove myself to the solitary wilds of the Connecticut Western Reserve where my former sins were unknown." There as "atonement for my transgressions" he "would found a town in that distant land." He would administer it on strict Christian principles. Maintaining it "under law and order, he would emphasize morality and promote education."

Hudson's re-conversion doubtless added a new dimension and inspiration to his enterprise in what he termed "the howling wilderness." But it did not prompt it: the idea of the undertaking and Hudson's part in it had been settled upon years before. Further, the township was acquired and Hudson's share in it established in January 1798. And four years before his "spiritual reawakening" he had bought "a one-thousandth part of the Reserve," paying $1,500 for it.

Everyone in the big Hudson House by the lake was up early. All preparations for Hudson's departure were in readiness. David Hudson was starting at dawn for that mysterious country across the mountains. He was leaving his wife and five young children. Like John Adams, who in 1778 had taken his ten-year-old son on his perilous voyage to France, Hudson was to be accompanied by his boy, Ira, who was eleven. The oldest child, Samuel, thirteen, was afflicted, probably retarded, although in the harsh vernacular of the day his father was to label him "crazy." We can imagine Anna, overlooking the scene from the doorway, holding baby Abigail Laura whimpering in her arms, while Timothy who was three clung timidly to his mother's skirts. William, ten, and Milo, a year younger, prancing about, would have envied Ira his good luck. There is no record of how Anna felt.

Hudson kept a detailed journal of his trip. This factual, unembellished record is a documentary on the settlement of Connecticut's Western Reserve. He had hired two Goshen men as helpers and en route was to engage several more, some at fifty cents a day. One of them was Joseph Darrow, an influential man who was much relied upon by Hudson. The chilly, laggard sun soon broke over the East. Ragged patches of snow, remnants of Connecticut's bitter winter, lingered in the hedgerows as the party crossed from Connecticut into New York State and headed for the Albany Road. Hudson's immediate destination was Nathaniel Norton's farm near present-day East Bloomfield in New York State's Ontario County. The stretches of fertile plain they encountered, so different from Connecticut's landscape, seemed a promise of what lay ahead in the faraway land. As they plodded on, spring overtook them. Dogwood and shadbush powdered the tall forest trees with white. Clumps of golden cowslips glowed in the marshlands, and the mud made the roads almost impassable.

Finally they turned in at Norton's gate. With Hudson and Birdsey, Nathaniel Norton was a proprietor and the third member of the "Company" controlling Reserve's Township 4. His farm was to be the launching pad and supply center for all the company's expeditions to the Ohio country even though he was never to see that land. He had bought 350 acres here in New York two years before, paying fifty cents an acre for what was once part of the vast Phelps-Gorham Tract.

Nathaniel operated a busy trading post with Birdsey, an absentee partner, who maintained his home in Goshen. Nathaniel also managed mills and a profitable distillery. Blooded livestock, offspring of herds he had driven overland from Goshen, roamed his fields. His log house was of ample size to accommodate his family and the wayfarers as well.

Hudson remained at Nathaniel's place for eleven days while he and his men collected supplies: quantities of potatoes, pork, bread, cheese, chocolate, sugar. Optimistically bags of wheat and corn were included for crops in the new land. He gathered a variety of tools, axes, plowshares, fishing tackle, blankets, heavy shoes. One cow worth $30 and another valued at $20 were listed as well as Morse's *Geography* and 31¾ gallons of whisky from Norton's distillery.

En route Hudson met Benjamin Tappan, headed for a neighboring township (Tappan's was the future Ravenna). They decided to join forces for part of the way. Their combined livestock was dispatched overland in the charge of their hired men. Ira went with this contingent. Their instructions were to follow "the paths of the Savages" as indicated on a crude map they were given.

As planned, Hudson and the rest of the group were to come by water via Lake Ontario and Lake Erie. The route was considered not only the most direct, but most desirable since it avoided possible Indian encounters via land. With his supplies assembled, Hudson hurried his party to Irondequoit Bay, the Ontario port where the Genesee River empties its waters ("Jerundagut" in Hudson's journal). To his dismay he found the boats he had made provision for were unseaworthy. After sending his men back for replacements, Hudson finally got his group under way, "rowing in open boats with no power but muscles of the arm and good whiteoak oars."

They encountered continual difficulties. At Niagara to their astonishment they found the river choked with floating ice. Blocked also by twelve-foot sheets of ice, they were forced with the greatest effort to portage their boats around the falls. They finally reached Buffalo, and once into Lake Erie they came upon calm, clear water. But a heavy rolling swell developed, delaying them several days. Although they arrived at Conneaut with a fair wind, it shifted without warning, blowing one of the heavily loaded barges against the rocky shore where it filled quickly with water. Several days were spent trying to salvage some of the food and attempting to repair the battered craft. In a final calamity thieves plundered one of the boats, making off with their precious supply of pork, their whisky, flour, and considerable other fare.

With food supplies dangerously low, Hudson worried that his men "faced famine." With the prospect of not enough supplies to see them through the venture, he considered turning back and abandoning the entire undertaking. Instead, after a sleepless night, he determined on a daring move: he would appropriate some of the flour in a consignment belonging to Eliphalet Austin, founder of Austinburg in the Reserve's future Ashtabula County, and promptly send payment to him there.

Cleveland, under the hill, as drawn by Allen Gaylord, 1800.
Courtesy of the Western Reserve Historical Society.

Finally, miraculously surviving their ordeals, on June 10 they rowed triumphantly from Lake Erie into the mouth of the Cuyahoga River. They were welcomed by Lorenzo Carter, the first settler in what was to be the City of Cleveland. From his cabin home that did duty also as an inn and trading post, Carter had been watching their approach. He helped them reassemble and provided them with a sturdy replacement for their much-weakened boat.

Hudson's map indicated he was within twenty-five miles of his township. He decided to row up the Cuyahoga with part of his equipment. The water, however, was so shallow that he was forced to disembark at Brandywine Falls (near present-day Northfield).

An old photograph of the falls of the Brandywine.

He was near his township, he knew. Day after day he hacked his way through the seemingly endless bogs, fighting gnats and countless other insects as he hunted for the surveyor's marker that designated it. "And all the while," he confided in his journal, "most heartily repenting ever having undertaken the expedition."

On the eve of the seventh day he stumbled on what he sought. It was June 17, 1799, the forty-eighth day since he had left Goshen. Greatly to Hudson's relief, a loud halloing and crashing of the

underbrush heralded the long-overdue arrival of the men with Ira
and the cattle. One can imagine the exchange of experiences that
ensued. But the factual Hudson mentioned nothing of this in his
journal.

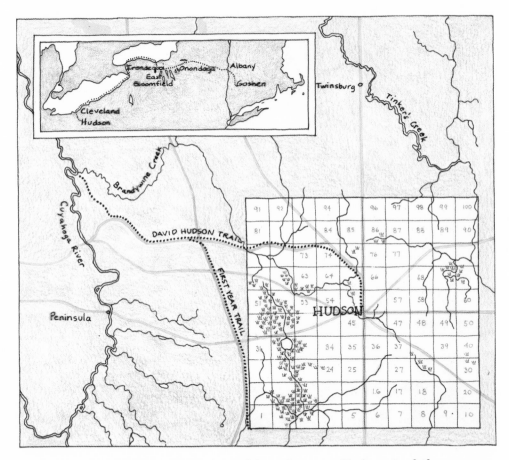

A few days before, Hudson, taking time to climb out of the swamp,
had found that a broad stretch of level ground lay beyond. A crude
road soon was hacked out through the marsh, a rough landsled
fashioned, and the oxen, straining every muscle, hauled the supplies

up to the high area. The rain that had drenched them for days subsided. Like a good omen the sun burst through scudding clouds, highlighting a pleasant country of forest and plain as far as eye could see. In their eager exploring they came upon a spring with a steady outpouring of clean, sweet water. Hoofprints indicated it was a favorite gathering place for forest animals. Hudson's chart showed he was in Great Lot 55 in the center of the township. "As darkness fell," he wrote, "I lodged here under an oak tree with grateful pleasure in resting on my own land."

His men, who had been stricken earlier with the ague, now were recovering and the all-important surveying went ahead with dispatch. The village-to-be was mapped out roughly after the plan of Connecticut towns around a central open area. The land donated and later enlarged by Hudson eventually became a typical Connecticut village green.

On a rise of ground near the spring, the towering trees were cut down, a superhuman achievement for men depending only on hand-manipulated axes and physical strength. But the forest monarchs came crashing to the earth, shattering the forest stillness. Promptly work began on building a substantial cabin with the fallen logs. Amidst the tree stumps in the clearing around this "first house in the Village" the men planted wheat and corn brought from home.

With the autumn haze creeping over the landscape and the leaves a blaze of October color, it was time for Hudson to head for home. Accompanied by Ira and one of the hired hands, he followed the same route as before, encountering even worse hazards. The hired men were left to spend the winter in the new cabin in charge of the wilderness domain. Food and generous supplies of drink were laid in, with plenty of shot to guarantee a rich supplemental diet from the abundant wild game.

W.L. TAYLOR.

HUDSON'S FIRST SETTLERS ARRIVE

DAVID HUDSON with his son Ira and a hired man reached Goshen in November 1799. As he was to return to the West in January a busy interlude confronted him. He submitted his report to Birdsey Norton. Expenses for the trip and for laying out the town had come to $300. Doubtless Birdsey was also interested in learning about the new land that he and his brother Nathaniel had acquired in the Western Reserve across the mountains. On his next trip Hudson was to take his wife, Anna, and their six living children. Arrangements had to be made for disposal of their home, and he was to recruit settlers for his wilderness domain.

While Hudson was in Goshen the slowly circulating news reached the town of Washington's death the latter part of December. The country was plunged into mourning for the man who had been its father figure for as long as most citizens could remember. He indeed had been, in the words of Henry Lee, "first in war, first in peace, and first in the hearts of his countrymen."

Doubtless at this time Hudson concluded the arrangement with the Nortons by which he acquired one-fourth interest in the township. The agreement was filed the end of January in the Litchfield County Court House. Also at this time one-eighth share of the township was purchased by Benjamin Oviatt, Stephen Baldwin, and Theodore Parmele, the deed issued a few months later.

Hudson proved to be a good salesman of his Reserve lands. He met with widespread interest and soon had gathered a handpicked lot of neighbors and friends who were ready to leave with him. They were the vanguard of a steadily increasing stream from this area who would stamp the new settlement as a Connecticut transplant. Joel Gaylord was returning, accompanied this time by a relative, Ruth Gaylord. Dr. Moses Thompson was coming, commissioned by his father to look over land for all of the family. Heman Oviatt, Benjamin's son, was ready for the adventure and would have a leading role in the new settlement. There were also the Samuel Bishops with four sons, a couple with an infant in arms, and three Vermonters who joined en route but did not remain in the township.

The party and their hired men, making a sizeable group, left Goshen in open sleighs, and like an introduction to the rigors ahead, encountered bitter cold, heavy snow, and near impassable roads. Following the same route as Hudson had taken the previous year, they were to stop at Nathaniel Norton's in New York State, and like Hudson would travel from there on Lake Ontario and Lake Erie. Norton welcomed them all, housing some in his home, the big main cabin, the others in an auxiliary structure built to accommodate the increasing number of west-going settlers passing through this part of the state. They gathered gratefully at cabin hearths, their chill soon dispatched before the roaring fires fed by plentiful logs from the Norton woodlot. Both cabins were equipped with beds, apparently enough for all the travelers. The beds were arranged in tiers, each one pegged into the wall packet-boat fashion.

Hudson's contingent remained there for many weeks—until the ice began to disappear in Lake Ontario. With twenty-nine individuals as well as quantities of freight to transport, Hudson needed a flotilla of eight boats. Work began at once on building the batteux, the local name for the flat-bottomed type used there since first fashioned the previous century by Indian traders. They had followed the early French missionaries like Father Hennepin who paddled over the streams in Indian canoes. Since that day the region had become a center for building the sturdy vessels. Enterprising Nathaniel Norton had seen to it that his outpost had its share of the pioneer industry. Thus Hudson was assured his boats were in the hands of experts and noted with satisfaction the piles of well-cured lumber that Norton had at hand—green wood was unacceptable as it soaked up water.

David Hudson was overseeing all preparations and at the same time giving attention to gathering provisions and a quantity of miscellaneous supplies. It was a long list: window glass for the cabin he had built at the settlement, bolts of woolen and linen cloth, such seeds as peach, cherry, and fennel as well as potatoes and onions for planting in the new land. He acquired numerous tools to augment those he had taken with him before. A scythe, an augur, a couple of adzes and tobacco and whisky—provisions enough, he hoped, to last a year. Fourteen cows were rounded up as well as hogs, a bull, a horse, and a yoke of oxen. His total expenditure came to about $2,000—a large sum for that time, but handled in part at least as company expense. The animals were to be driven overland by the young Bishops, but the people and the commodities had to go by water. To build the number of boats called for was a major undertaking and work went ahead from early morning until darkness.

The months passed. Warmer weather was taking over. Norton's forest trees were beginning to leaf, and at their feet early wildflowers sprinkled the ground with color. With the ice breaking up in the lake, preparations to depart were under way and the accumulated cargo, loaded on a flat boat, was drayed by oxen to Irondequoit Bay.

Ready to sail at daybreak the voyagers assembled and slept the night before in a clearing near the water. Hudson, suddenly overcome with realization of the responsibility he had assumed, could not rest. Confiding his feelings to his journal, he wrote: "While my dear wife and my children and all those men and women were sleeping around me, I could not close my eyes." He began to think about the danger they all faced "in crossing the boisterous lakes," and the possibility they "might fall before the Indians' tomahawks," but finally "appealing to Israel's God," he committed them all "to His care, went to sleep and was ready to launch out in the morning on the Great Deep."

His apprehension was justified. Reading the journal today one wonders how the travelers lived through the lake storms, or why they chose the water route in the first place. In the early going, the weather was fairly propitious with no real difficulties confronting them until they reached Lake Erie. Gale winds then buffeted the boat that was carrying most of the settlers, finally slamming the craft onto a sand bar. It filled at once with water threatening everyone on board with drowning until suddenly a powerful wave floated it free. A couple of miles further on, near their destination, they camped on the bank of the Cuyahoga, hoping to dry out. But a heavy rain descended and continued for five days. The water level rose alarmingly and everyone was drenched again. After waiting until they could row against the swollen river current, they got under way.

On May 28 they finally reached the landing that Hudson had built the year before in the lowland at the river's edge. As they disembarked the drivers with the livestock appeared. Impatient to learn about his men left in charge during the winter, Hudson commandeered a horse and hurried off on his mission.

He found his men in good spirits, heartily glad to see him, and appreciative of the shelter afforded by the snug cabin. Around it they pointed to the corn and wheat they had planted, which was beginning to put up tiny shoots amidst the stumps. Beyond, they had set out several rows of potatoes, turnips, and onions from their stores. Hudson now took time to inspect other parts of his land and was a couple of days getting back.

With the weather turned warm and humid, the women and children waiting on the landing had been attacked by continuing swarms of mosquitoes and gnats. Hudson found them with eyes swollen shut, faces covered with welts, children crying, and the women bewailing ever having come to this wild country. It was unfortunate that at this moment a hired man came up to report that one of the oxen had collapsed, weakened by insect bites.

At once taking charge, Hudson led the sorry group out of the swampy lowland to high ground where the great trees offered pleasant shade, and as they moved on into the open country the air grew balmy and refreshing—and there were no mosquitoes. Recent miseries seem soon to have been forgotten.

Even the afflicted ox had revived. The men began transferring the supplies from the boats to flat boats drayed by the oxen to the clearing, a challenging task even for these beasts. With the cargo disposed of Hudson gathered everyone for "a service of Thanksgiving and praise to Almighty God for bringing them safely through the perils of the voyage." For the service he selected an open area in what would become part of the west green. As they rose from prayer and dusted off their knees, one of the men declared that the new town should be called Hudson. And loud agreement was echoed by everyone.

The Fourth of July soon was upon them—the twenty-fourth anniversary of the Declaration of Independence that had changed world history. Except for the very young among them, all had lived through the Revolutionary War. Some, like Joel Gaylord who had been a drummer boy at the Battle of Monmouth, were veterans of the war. Plainly it was a day to be celebrated. A section in the heart of the township that Hudson had set aside as part of the green was the location for the festivities. A feast was called for. Tables were improvised with poles laid across notched logs and covered with layers of elm bark. Wild turkey, venison, squirrel stew, pigeon pie, and other delectable game were served. The women supplied quantities of corn bread from their scant supplies. Wild berries sweetened with generous amounts of honey plundered from hollow bee trees made the dessert. And hearty toasts were drunk in whisky.

Heman Oviatt presided as master of ceremonies. Hudson distributed a half of a bag of shot to every man with a rifle for a marksman contest, the target a venerable shagbark hickory tree. A salvo from thirteen guns honored the thirteen colonies and a spirited chorus on a blacksmith's anvil won loud applause. The Declaration of Independence was read, every word of it, by Dr. Thompson whose father, Stephen, had been in several engagements during the long war. David Hudson gave the oration of the day.

People from surrounding settlements came by ox cart and horseback to attend the gathering. They brought their children who, joining the local boys and girls, were soon playing together as if longtime acquaintances. For the parents the contact with other strangers in this strange land proved to be a heartening and reassuring experience. David Hudson, aware of the benefit to his people from such associations, decided the day's program had been worth the effort.

Three months later Hudson's cabin, equipped with its real glass windows, had a new occupant: Anna Hudson gave birth to her eighth child, a girl. She named her Anner Maria for her mother back in Goshen in the Norton family home on Pie Hill. The little baby was the first white child born in what was to become Summit County. She grew up to be an able, much-admired woman, displaying many of the talents of her father. On her ninetieth birthday the entire town staged a celebration in her honor.

In the year 1800 David Hudson and all settlers in the Western Reserve greatly benefited by passage of the Quieting Act. Until enactment of this legislation purchasers of property in the Reserve had no deed or title to their land. Since its acquisition by Connecticut the Reserve had been administered from Hartford in the same way the colonies had been ruled from London. With passage of the act, Connecticut was required to release jurisdiction to the United States of all claims to the lands drawn in the drafts, and thus the untenable situation was corrected. General Arthur St. Clair, governor of the Northwest Territory, then created a county to contain all the Western Reserve. He named it Trumbull, honoring Governor Jonathan Trumbull of Connecticut. For the county seat he designated a new settlement that he called Warren in honor of General Moses Warren, Revolutionary War veteran of Lyme, Connecticut. And so it was that on a hot summer day in 1800 the first county court session was held in Warren in a shady spot between two corncribs. From the start Warren forged ahead, soon becoming the political and industrial center of this part of the Reserve.

John Marshall, President Adams's secretary of state, had been influential in passage of the Quieting Act, and as one of Adams's last official acts he named Marshall chief justice of the Supreme Court.

. . . AND A
NEW TOWN CAME INTO BEING

MORE SETTLERS WERE arriving. Sometimes a couple of families in a single day. The early nineteenth-century movement from eastern America was reaching the Ohio country. "The inexorable, age-old push westward," it has been called, "the drift of humankind eternally seeking the always vanishing frontier." People were coming overland now, in covered wagons with their kettles and pots and pans and a few precious mementoes from the home many would never see again.

They halted their weary oxen at David Hudson's cabin. There, with their tired children whimpering at their knees, they pored over his crude maps locating what was to be their land in this big lonely

wilderness. Climbing back into their clumsy wagons they followed him as he saddled his horse and led them to their acres over rough girdled trails through the forest, the endless forest. They did not yet realize that the giant trees, such an impressive evidence of this new land's fertility, would become their first challenge as they attacked them with ax and muscle to clear the land for farming.

As they jogged along, the sky might darken with a great congregation of wild pigeons passing overhead, shattering the stillness with the roar of their wings. Or they might hear the far-off eerie cry from a wild beast of the forest, one of the creatures that had survived the Indians' arrows but would succumb to the white man's bullet. Perhaps Hudson could point to a plume of smoke rising in the distant treetops, the heartening banner from some other newcomer's cabin. If they came in the spring there would be the cheery color of wildflowers to greet them and hurrying brooks with abundant clear water. But no roads. No near neighbors. Nobody except themselves, and Squire Hudson, their ombudsman.

The census took an encouraging spurt early in 1801 with the arrival of Heman Oviatt, his wife, Eunice, and their two boys who came with the Joel Gaylords and their three sons and five daughters. The two families traveled by way of Pittsburgh, following buffalo and Indian trails, chopping their way through brush and woodland, somehow negotiating the unbridged rivers. The men had put up a shanty in the village when they had come with David Hudson the previous year. Here they now housed their families, grateful for the shelter until cabins could be built.

Oviatt's land, over three hundred acres, gift of his father, Benjamin, lay a mile or so to the south of the village. Gaylord's was a larger tract, part of which he later donated to make the northwest quadrant of the village green. Hudson had known Oviatt in Goshen. In fact they both had been "born again" at the Reverend Asahel Hooker's revival meeting.

On his first trip Oviatt had prepared a four-acre clearing and planted wheat he had brought from home. It was a fine crop now, but not yet ripe. Hudson, however, had a little grain garnered from somewhere. Oviatt undertook to get it to the only mill in the area, the one at Newburgh, twenty-five miles distant. With the wheat in his ox cart, his horse tied on behind, he set out over what passed for roads, made worse by the spring thaw, and reached the mill twelve hours later. Oviatt and his family were short of food, he tells us in his reminiscences, and as he had planned, he left Hudson's grain and his oxen at the mill and headed on horseback for Rocky River where he had heard the fishing was good.

"I crossed the Cuyahoga [River] in a canoe," he wrote, "swam my horse and at Rocky River fished for two nights with a spear and caught a barrel of Pike." Back at the mill "I salted my Fish in a Flower barrel, bought half a barrel of Pork, took Hudson's grist, my Pork and fish, and went home rich in provisions."

The Oviatt land was near the old Indian trail referred to as the Stigmanish Trail for the fine old Seneca chief. Remnants of this tribe and of the Ottawas and Chippewas lingered in the area ignoring the treaty by which the majority had been moved west. The Indians frequently stopped at the Oviatt cabin and soon Heman developed a lively trade with them.

Before long he was carrying furs and pelts packsaddle to Pittsburgh, the nearet market for products of the forest, and a long, hazardous journey. He set up a distillery on his farm and paid the tribesmen in whisky: half a pint for a coonskin, one pint for a buckskin, up the scale to four quarts for a good bearskin. Oviatt opened a store on Main Street (the Cleveland Road). It was a crude log structure, but the first store in the village. He soon was able to stock it with shawls, calico, thread, needles, and pins bartered in Pittsburgh for his furs, and greatly appreciated by Hudson villagers. Whisky also available at his store attracted loitering Indians, soon boisterous and unruly from too much of it.

Eunice Oviatt, her husband's aggressive business aid, mastered several tribal dialects, and while it was claimed she could drive as hard a bargain with the Indians as her husband, she was kind to them. She gained their confidence and never had any trouble with them. Hudson pioneer annals, however, record numerous incidents when the Indians, especially when fired by drink, menaced lonely cabins, frightening women and children. But on the whole the Indians were peaceable, due in a large measure to David Hudson's effort from the first to develop friendly contacts with the tribes, joining in conferences with them, giving them practical help, and always welcoming the tall, dignified Chief Stigmanish to his cabin. In contrast to the usual settler's point of view that the Indians' lands were there to be seized, Hudson was disturbed by the white man's treatment of these first Americans.

Before long David Hudson had a new title, justice of the peace. He had written to the august General Arthur St. Clair, recently named governor of the Northwest Territory, asking to be named to this office in Hudson Township. St. Clair probably never had heard of the writer or of his town, but Hudson nevertheless won the appointment in 1801 and filled it for twenty-five years.

Shortly, the justice was called upon in his official capacity. It had been love at first sight between the newly arrived settlers, Olive Gaylord and George Darrow, and it would be Justice Hudson's function to marry them. Nervous about his initial performance, he told his wife about it, admonishing her to keep it a secret. Anna, however, could not resist sharing the exciting news with just one friend who likewise was to tell no other person. On the designated day the justice headed for the Gaylord cabin in a roundabout route through the woods, hoping thus to camouflage his errand. Imagine his surprise when he arrived to find every settler in the township, including his wife, assembled to celebrate the little community's first wedding.

Joel Gaylord sold his new son-in-law two and one-half acres of his large holdings for $80.00 and gave his daughter, probably as her dowry, another piece. He stipulated it was not to be taken over by her husband but was to remain in her name and in her control. Joel, in short, an early advocate of women's rights, did not hold with the then current notion that once a woman married, her husband had complete authority over her property.

Shortly after the wedding the justice set up court in his crowded cabin. In his journal he recorded that he meted out fines of from $1.25 to $2.00 for transgressions like "provoking affrays"—meaning drunken brawls? Nor did he demur when confronted with an unpleasant duty such as "Issuing a warrant for a certain prominent citizen who had gotten the minor daughter of another prominent citizen with child."

More settlers this year. Dr. Moses Thompson came heading a cavalcade of ox carts and a two-horse hitch pulling a heavily loaded covered wagon. A string of farm animals plodded along behind including two cows for the milk supply en route. The young doctor was returning after his first visit the previous year, now bringing his family, his parents, and his brothers and their families. Last year he had walked back to Connecticut carrying a precious gift of $50.00 the enterprising Squire Hudson had given him for the purchase of medicines. It was by way of inducement for his return and permanent residence as caretaker of the new town's people.

The Thompsons had been six weeks on the way. The doctor's father, the devout Stephen Thompson senior, insisted that all travel halt on the Lord's Day for Bible reading and prayer—by the side of the road on a fair day, otherwise with all of them crowded into what passed for inns. En route the Thompsons met the George Kilbournes and the two groups came along together for a time. Kilbourne had sold his Goshen farm to Birdsey Norton, who was buying real estate, a program he was to follow through the years. Kilbourne brought along one hundred books he had assembled in Goshen with the help of his pastor, the Reverend Asahel Hooker. Once he was settled he organized his books as a "district library," selling shares in it to

readers throughout the township. Although no list exists of the books
in this the first Hudson library, the family statement can be accepted
that "the subjects dealt with Morality and Religion."

The town lacked that essential pioneer industry, a mill. There was
still only the one at Newburgh, a three-day round trip by ox cart.
So it was at Newburgh that the settlement's first harvest was
processed, the wheat David Hudson had planted on his nine acres
during his first visit. He recorded the story in his journal, February
1801. The milling yielded 183 bushels, he noted. Thaddeus Lacey,
who had accompanied Hudson on that first trip, was given one-fourth
of the grain for harvesting and threshing, and Hudson received one-
fourth. The remainder was sold locally, the proceeds credited as
follows: five-eighths to Birdsey and Nathaniel Norton; one-eighth to
the joint account of Benjamin Oviatt, Theodore Parmele, and Stephen
Baldwin. This modest but precious first product of the land, in other
words, was allocated to the town's shareholders in proportion to the
investment of each—company members, the Nortons and Hudson,
getting seven-eighths, while one-eighth went to the three recent
"tenants in common." It is a revealing glimpse of frontier financial
practice and of David Hudson's careful bookkeeping.

After many unsuccessful efforts to establish a local mill, Hudson
finally persuaded two young men, Aaron Norton and Ezra Wyatt,
to put up two mills, one for lumber and one a grist mill. They were
built in the extreme northeastern part of the township at Tinker's
Creek on the Hudson-Aurora Road.

It was a difficult undertaking and the mills were ill-fated first
and last. Straight off the young millers-to-be struck quicksand.
Hudson characteristically met the emergency. In his daybook he
notes: "Have engaged to make Aaron Norton a free gift of 100 acres
to encourage him to go on with the mills after discovery of

quicksand." He adds that he has "been at the expense of furnishing all Wyatt's provisions, laborers and all things necessary to build ½ of the mills, and to take my pay in bonds due one, two, three and four years hence without interest."

Hudson was putting up a barn, a large one across the Cleveland Road from his cabin near where in a few years he would erect his house. The barn was built of black walnut. The boards, which would be worth a small fortune today, were fashioned at the Tinker's Creek site. He credited the milling cost toward what the young men owed him.

The mills served not only Hudson settlers but those in surrounding townships. A distillery was installed. They were much patronized and all went well for two years. Then a fire broke out, destroying the entire operation.

Some time later the mills were rebuilt but did not last long. Nothing at the site now suggests that the busy mills ever existed. Today's motorist, driving over the smart new roadway bridge there is scarcely aware of gentle Tinker's Creek below, quietly channeling itself through tangles of brush and tall grasses, the unpretentious heir of a once mighty watercourse.

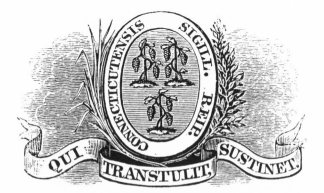

Joseph Badger.

SALVATION IN A SADDLEBAG

ONE DAY IN 1802 a courier from Warren brought a most heartening communication to Squire Hudson: the Trumbull County Commissioners had voted that his settlement was to be made a township. It would include Stow, Aurora, Boston, and Mantua, attached to it temporarily for administrative convenience. Accordingly in April twenty men designated as electors from Hudson and the other four settlements, gathered at the Hudson cabin to crowd into the room and sit as best they could elbow to elbow on a row of benches. After a chairman was chosen—Squire Hudson unanimously won the honor—they elected other officers: Lacey as clerk, Oviatt and Abraham Thompson as trustees; they also appointed fence viewers and supervisors of what they optimistically called highways. It was voted that Hudson would be the name of the township. This first political meeting had a full agenda and business lasted well into the night.

In mid-summer Hudson returned to Goshen, the first of numerous trips. Travel to and from Connecticut seems to have been no problem to these hardy pioneers. This time he was going overland, on horseback. After about fifty miles his mount was so weakened by attacks of gnats and other insects that it could go no further. Hudson sold the animal and, apparently sturdier than the horse, swung his pack on his back and walked to Nathaniel Norton's place at East Bloomfield. There he procured another horse and rode the rest of the way to Goshen.

He found his property that was for sale was not moving. This was the case with other Goshen homesites vacated by owners who like Hudson had joined the cavalcade for New Connecticut. The west-going trend, steadily increasing, was beginning to show its effect with a farm here and there abandoned to weeds, and houses standing vacant and uncared for.

Hudson carrying out his three-fold function in the new settlement as manager of the "Company," a member of it, and owner of many acres of its land, had reports to submit to Birdsey and Nathaniel as absentee managers of township affairs. For his part Hudson kept careful account of his responsibilities in the joint ownership, and a glance at these records reveals a good deal about Hudson as the meticulous businessman. "To myself from April 22 to November 18, 1799," one report began, "for superintending New Connecticut settlers, $.53." Another entry: "have expended much time in doing business with writing, reviewing, rucking [making roads], in going to the Indians, trading with them and giving them presents."

Not only what he spent, but money he had received was accounted for. He had "boarded Lacey's three children for 12½ weeks for $13 at $1.10 a week." Heman Oviatt paid $10.84 for nine days' board while a cup of cider cost Joel Gaylord five cents.

The Nortons, in turn, had a claim: "a final settlement for the expense of surveying and settling the town of Hudson a ballance . . . is due the Company from David Hudson for one quarter of the whole expense . . . of which Hudson's share is $21.04." With payment Hudson would be "entitled to one quarter part of the movable property belonging to the Company." This memorandum was signed by Birdsey Norton "for myself and Nathaniel Norton."

While in Goshen Hudson took time "to make a purchase of books to the value of $100.00," he records in his journal. Like Kilbourne he distributed them as a circulating library not only in the settlement but in neighboring villages as well. It is claimed "they were very useful in forming and enlightening the minds of many youth."

On a warm September day, not long after David's Hudson homecoming, a mud-spattered weary horseman and an equally exhausted animal clattered into the squire's dooryard. The rider, the Reverend Joseph Badger, carried the Word of God in his saddlebag, and an ax to cut his way through the wilderness. He was one of the indefatigable preachers sent out by the Connecticut Missionary Society to bring the message of Christ to the New West. Originally their aims had been to Christianize the heathen Indians, but now their responsibilities were more and more with the growing number of unchurched settlers throughout the frontier. For many months Badger had been crisscrossing New Connecticut, floundering on "floorboards" over swollen streams, menaced by wild beasts and lost many nights in the trackless forests. En route to Hudson he and his horse had been waylaid by a growling black bear. As the animal bared its teeth and prepared to attack, Badger quickly boosted himself high up in a sturdy tree. He clung to his lofty perch through the night to be drenched shortly by a violent rain and windstorm. The bear and the horse kept vigil at the foot of the tree until morning when the grizzly ambled off and the rider and horse proceeded on their way.

A Revolutionary War veteran, Badger had enlisted at eighteen immediately after Lexington. Surviving British bullets, the Continental army's issues of inadequate clothing and starvation rations, he was laid low in an almost fatal smallpox attack. When peace came, he entered Yale to pepare for the ministry. Now as a missionary he worked under the ecumenical Plan of Union by which Presbyterians and Congregationalists operated jointly in the sparsely populated frontier where resources were inadequate to support two separate denominations. Although Badger was a Presbyterian he conscientiously maintained a consistent "Presbygational" stance, thus avoiding any denominational controversy.

One of David Hudson's early projects had been to put up a cabin on the south green. He planned it would serve as a church on Sunday and a school on weekdays. It was a crude little structure, probably outfitted with uncomfortable backless benches. But it was the first church building and the first schoolhouse in what became Summit County. Hudson took charge of the Sunday services, soon gaining the title deacon.

On the Sabbath a few days after his arrival Badger preached in the little church. Considering that he had trained at Yale where its president Timothy Dwight was the eloquent apostle of John Calvin, he doubtless subscribed to the dour creed of predestination, the belief that for man, innately a sinner, life was an ante-chamber to the bliss of heaven after death, or to eternal torment in the fires of hell. All depended upon whether or not he had sought—and found—salvation in his lifetime. While Bagder seems to have held a somewhat gentler version, it was essentially the Calvinism Hudson settlers had brought with them from Connecticut. There that theology dominated religious thought and prompted frequent revival meetings like the one where Hudson found salvation on the eve of his departure to the Ohio country. Thus as Badger besought his listeners to seek Christ and God's grace, he was understood and welcomed by this handful of "eagerly pious people," as he referred to them.

Drawing by Henry Howe from *Historical Collections of Ohio*.
THE OLD CHURCH

Badger recorded in his *Memoir* that, on a memorable September day, "I organized the church in that place [Hudson], the Calvinistic Congregational Church." Thirteen joined, including David Hudson, Stephen Thompson and wife, George and Almira Kilbourne, Heman Oviatt and wife, Hannah Lindly, and Amos Lusk. All but the last two had been members of the Reverend Hooker's Congregational church in Goshen. David Hudson, it appears, had been preparing for some time for this event. Goshen church records indicate that a year before "the Church voted [probably at Hudson's request] a certificate of regular standing to the eleven, all removed from us to the Town of Hudson in New Connecticut."

The Hudson church was the second one organized in the Reserve. Badger had dedicated the first the previous year in Austinburg. He also had established his family in that settlement. His cabin was built "with half a floor of split logs and half of dirt." It had no chimney and there were "cracks between the logs and no plastering or mudding." He supported his wife and six children on his missionary salary of seven dollars a week. In 1803 the devout officials of the Missionary Society, indifferent to their agent's earthly needs, reduced his pay to six dollars. He remonstrated that he could not take care of his family on this amount, but his protest went unheeded. "I concluded," he wrote, "to go on as I had done, and trust in Him who feeds the ravens."

He frequently stopped in Newburgh where "infidelity and profaning the Sabbath are general" and where despite all he could do "they did fair to grow into a hardened, corrupt society." From Newburgh he usually headed his horse to Hudson, "more than twenty miles distant, a lonely tour in the cold, snow and mud." But once arrived he was sure of a cordial reception. Everyone in the settlement came to sit through his morning and afternoon sermons, always long and always emphasizing man's depravity and his need to seek salvation.

From time to time other itinerant missionaries stopped in Hudson, taking over the church program. But the responsibility for maintaining regular services fell to Deacon Hudson, and he is said never to have missed a Sunday.

True to their heritage, Hudson and Badger endorsed education almost as fervently as religion. In Goshen before leaving on his last trip, Hudson and his associates had drawn up a deed allocating 160 acres—lot 91—in the extreme northwestern part of the township for the support of local schools. Now, less than two years later, Hudson and Badger were dreaming of a college for this part of the Reserve— a Yale of the West to train pioneers' sons as preachers for the local churches they felt certain were to come. They daringly petitioned the territorial legislature for a charter. Their appeal was refused, but neither man gave up the idea. They had to wait, however, for its realization until 1826 when Western Reserve College was founded in Hudson. By that time Badger was an established minister in Gustavus, Trumbull County.

On September 4, 1952, the sesquicentennial of Hudson's first church and schoolhouse, a great boulder was placed on the green where the original church had stood. A bronze plaque affixed to the stone memorialized the little structure built one hundred and fifty years before. The project was the joint undertaking of the Hudson Congregational Church and the Hudson Library and Historical Society.

THE BACONS

ANOTHER CONNECTICUT MISSIONARY, the Reverend David Bacon, arrived in Hudson in 1804. With him were his wife, Alice, their two-year-old son Leonard, and an infant of six weeks. They had come from the northern Michigan wilderness near the Straits of Mackinac where they had been sent by the Connecticut Missionary Society to carry Christianity to the Ojibway Indians. After four heartbreaking years struggling with insufficient funds and the indifference of the Indians to Calvinism's stern precepts, the Bacons gathered up their children, born at the outpost, and left.

David Hudson, who had known the family "back home,"

REVEREND DAVID BACON

welcomed them and somehow found space for them in the cabin already overtaxed with seven young Hudsons, two hired hands, and often a waylaid traveler or two. Since the departure of the Reverend Joseph Badger, the squire, as "Deacon" Hudson, had taken charge of the Sabbath Day services in the little church on the green, an undertaking that was becoming a burden in his increasingly busy life. Now he proposed that Bacon assume that responsibility, dividing his time between work for the church and missionary labors in other parts of the Reserve. He would receive $136 a year from the village congregation, and the missionary, his wife, and children would have room and board with the Hudsons for $2 a week. Bacon accepted what must have seemed a God-sent turn of events.

Before Bacon could begin the program, a letter from mission headquarters caught up with him. The pious officials ordered him to Hartford to account for his failure with the Indians, his poor management of his dollar and ten cents a day salary and of the money allowed him for mission expenses. Distraught and feeling the expense of a horse for the journey not justified, Bacon started out in a November sleet storm and walked to Connecticut, arriving the latter part of December. After prayerful consideration by the mission hierarchy, his accounts were found to be in order and his missionary salary restored. Exonerated, Bacon walked back to Hudson. Reaching there in March he began the schedule agreed upon.

Drawing from P. P. Cherry's *Western Reserve and Early Ohio.*

After long agitation a postal route had been granted the village, and Squire Hudson was appointed postmaster. With the new demands on the cabin, plainly an auxiliary structure was called for, and one went up quickly a little to the east of the original. The first night the family occupied it, they were awakened by the glare and crackle of flames bursting from the old cabin; its "cat and clay" chimney had become overheated, igniting the roof. Hudson's business papers and most of the family's belongings were still in the original cabin. Hudson was able to rescue his records but the children's clothes were destroyed. Loss of their shoes was a special problem as they could be replaced only by an itinerant cobbler whose visits were few and irregular.

Ever since a trip to Goshen when David had seen Birdsey Norton's big house under construction, he had been thinking about building a house for his own family. Now Anna was expecting another baby, and with the loss of the cabin, he decided to put up the house at

David Hudson's house from the north. Drawing by Horace Rogers.

once. Early in 1805 the work got under way. The site on the Cleveland Road, today's Main Street, was near the spring the squire had discovered when first taking possession of his land.

An ambitious undertaking, the house was to measure forty by thirty-two feet, with two full stories and a sizeable third for an attic. In the midst of simple log cabins it was to be of clapboard construction. Hudson had hoped to have the lumber prepared at the Tinker's Creek Mill on Aurora Road where boards were processed for the big barn he had built earlier. Since the mill was now destroyed, the logs had to be hauled to the Newburgh Mill, which would mean delay. Eager to have the house completed before the birth of the new baby, Hudson persuaded George Holcomb, his neighbor to the north, to help with the construction, delaying temporarily work on his own house that he had under way. But the baby, a boy, arrived September 5, and the house was not finished until early in 1806. The baby was christened David Hudson junior.

The house, of simple Federal design, reminiscent of those David knew in his homeland, stands today, the town's most treasured landmark.

Occupying a prominent place in the new house, a tall cherry chest fashioned by a local craftsman from trees on the farm, served as the post office. Letters, sent without envelopes or stamps, were franked, the fee usually paid by recipients. Until roads were passable for the stage, a man was dispatched on horseback at regular intervals to Cleveland and other points to collect the village mail.

Meanwhile David Bacon on his missionary travels came upon a township about ten miles south of Hudson that was newly opened for settlement. For some time he had dreamed of one day establishing a Utopian religious community exclusively for Congregationalists of sound Calvinistic conviction, and maybe a few God-fearing Presbyterians. The new township appealed to him as an ideal location.

The land, he found, was divided roughly into three sections, the largest controlled by Jonathan Brace and associates of Hartford, another by Ephraim Starr from Goshen, and the third by Colonel Benjamin Tallmadge of Litchfield. Brace and Starr were members of the Connecticut Land Company. The township eventually was to be named Tallmadge for the colonel, who had been aid-de-camp to General Washington during the war.

David Hudson's post office desk.
Portrait of Laura Hudson Oviatt.

Bacon gave up the program in Hudson and went to Connecticut leaving his family in Hudson where shortly their third child, a girl named Julia, was born. Bacon contracted for township acreage controlled by Tallmadge and Starr. No money, it appears, changed hands, the deals being based largely on a contract assumed by Bacon, mortgages on the land, and promissory notes. Income from sales to the expected settlers, it was assumed, would abrogate the debts.

Differing from the Connecticut town plan David Hudson had followed, the heart of Bacon's was a great central green with eight converging roads circling it. Each led like spokes of a wheel to the center where the church was to be. Negotiable in the era of oxen and horses, Tallmadge Circle is a challenge to today's rushing traffic swirling around it.

In the center near the site for the future church, Bacon had a cabin put up to be the home of his family. On a warm July day in 1807 a wagon drew up at David Hudson's door. Mrs. Bacon, cradling her new baby in her arms, climbed aboard. The rest of the family followed with their few possessions, and the oxen began the all-day ten-mile journey over the bumpy road to the lonely new home in the wilderness. One night shortly after they had come, Mrs. Bacon, alone in the cabin with her children, looked up to see an Indian, hands cupped to his eyes, looking in the window. Terrified, she pushed a chest against the door, blew out her candle, hushed her children, and sat in darkness until her husband's return.

Settlers trickled in slowly. In 1808 three families came. The next year the count rose to fourteen. Then more began coming, from Connecticut, from Vermont, and from settlements in the Reserve.

Jefferson's embargo of 1807, imposed after the British attack on the American frigate *Chesapeake*, however, was causing economic distress felt as far west as the Connecticut Western Reserve. With money hard to come by, settlers were falling behind in payment for their land and the proprietors were becoming concerned. In 1811 Bacon traveled to Connecticut where apparently he was able to reassure them, if only temporarily.

That year a little girl was born in the cabin at the center. Her mother named her Delia for her girlhood friend, Delia Ellsworth Williams, daughter of Chief Justice Oliver Ellsworth. One of this family, James W. Ellsworth, in the next century would turn Hudson, his birthplace, from a backward country village disheartened by a series of calamities into a vigorous modern town.

Mrs. Williams's namesake was to be one of the first—some claim *the* first—to promote the idea that the plays of Shakespeare were the work of Sir Francis Bacon (not related to Delia's family) and a brilliant coterie including Sir Walter Raleigh and Edmund Spenser. The group presumably used the Bard's name to cover certain irregular political activities.

Problems were increasing for Bacon. There was opposition to the two dollar annual property tax he had inserted in every deed "for support of the Congregational Calvinistic Order forever." Even less money was coming in now from the properties and there were few new settlers. Bacon was in difficulty. Not like his friend David Hudson, who was a good businessman, the visionary Bacon had been lax in management of township affairs and not always careful in record keeping. He had bought property at high prices and his debts were mounting. In 1812 the proprietors called him to Connecticut for a conference. He was encouraged at first, according to a letter he sent back to Tallmadge. But in the final decision he lost his contract.

He had been away several months and now returned a defeated, broken man. Nothing had been salvaged from his long dedication to the undertaking so deeply rooted in his Christian faith. Sadly he boarded up the little cabin and he and his family went back to Hartford. Two more children, sons, were born. In 1817 David Bacon died, age forty-six. He left his wife with a bevy of children and nothing for their support.

The town of Tallmadge survived, however. Contracts were readjusted and most of the original settlers remained, although in many cases they paid virtually twice for their farms. In the early decades of the nineteenth century Western migration fever was at its height, with Connecticut's Western Reserve especially attractive. Newcomers were moving into all parts of the township. Among the many from Connecticut was wealthy Elizur Wright who traded his farm at New Canaan for 3,000 acres in the township. On his first trip, in 1809, he had built a double log house on his land and returned the following year bringing his parents, his wife, their eight children, and two hired men. Their goods came in two covered wagons each drawn by two yoke of oxen. The family traveled in a covered carriage with a span of horses. The three groups kept together during the thirty-nine-day journey.

A brilliant mathematician at Yale, Wright was interested all his life in education and was the founder of the academy at Tallmadge. It was said he worked out complicated mathematical problems as he followed the plough on his farm. He was interested in the organization of Western Reserve College at Hudson and early became a trustee.

He may have become aware of the Tallmadge lands through acquaintance with Colonel Tallmadge. The colonel, who entertained President Washington in his Litchfield mansion, continued to dress as in the Revolutionary War era, powdered wig, satin trousers, and all.

After Bacon's death, his widow, Alice, reorganized her life and decided to open a millinery shop. Her son Leonard, who had graduated from Yale and launched in his life-career as a Congregational clergyman, loaned her six dollars for supplies. Delia was placed with Mrs. Williams. The thin little girl in tattered clothes cried for her mother. But she blossomed under her guardian's care, and in a few years was attending the best schools of the area.

Delia earned her living as a schoolteacher and in writing successful fiction, including a popular novel. She found her metier, however, as a speaker before drawing room literary groups, popular at the time. She soon gained a following of men as well as women attracted by her brilliance and charm. In studying Shakespeare, a frequent subject of her talks, she came upon ciphers and cryptograms from which she arrived at her idea about the authorship of the plays.

She decided to put her "findings" in a book and went to England for further study and work on it. Proving her theory became an obsession. She withdrew from the world, neglected her appearance and health, and gave all her energy to the undertaking. Finally the book was finished. Nathaniel Hawthorne, then American consul in Liverpool, wrote the preface although wholly rejecting the theme. The ponderous, six-hundred-page volume appeared as *The Philosophy of the Plays of Shakspere Unfolded*. And not a single critic had a good word to say for it. With the rejection of the work after her long concentration on it, her fine mind gave way.

In 1857, the year Delia's book appeared, Tallmadge, Ohio, by then a prosperous town of 2,500, was observing its semicentennial. The exercises took place in the Congregational church, one of the finest church edifices in Ohio. Largely credited to the master builder Lemuel Porter from Waterbury, Connecticut, it stood near the spot originally designated for a church by David Bacon, and in a real sense was a memorial to him. After the building was completed, Porter was summoned to Hudson where in 1826 he erected the first building on the new campus of Western Reserve College.

In the lengthy program that included Tallmadge reminiscences by local citizens, the featured speaker was Leonard Bacon, widely known

as the pastor of Hartford's First Congregational Church. He eulogized his father "whose prophetic vision saw the exquisite possibilities of this township." He described the trip from Hudson to the new cabin when he was a five-year-old boy. He spoke of his mother, often alone in the

cabin and afraid of the Indians with the nearest neighbor more than a mile away. But he made no mention of his sister's book, nor of Delia. She had been brought back to America by one of Leonard's sons, and was near death in a Hartford sanitarium.

OWEN BROWN

The Torrington, Connecticut birthplace of John Brown.

JOHN BROWN COMES TO HUDSON

SHORTLY AFTER David Hudson began to build his new house, John Brown, destined to become the village's most famous citizen, arrived in July 1805. He was five years old. He came with his parents from his birthplace, Torrington, Connecticut, a few miles from Goshen. His father, gaunt-faced Owen, not fully recovered from a bout with malaria, looked older than his thirty-four years. John's mother, Ruth, who at thirty-three had borne six children and lost two, was accorded a seat in the wagon, pulled by a slow ox team. For the entire tedious, jolting ride she held her baby, Oliver, and with the help of her seven-year-old daughter, Anna Ruth, looked after the lively, mischievous Salmon who was three

and chafed at the day after day confinement. Owen walked beside
the plodding oxen, urging them on with a sharp goad and his
monotonous, hoarse "Gee, Haw."

John rode their big horse some of the time, feeling very grown-up
on his high perch. More often he followed on foot with the Browns'
adopted son, Levi Blakeslee, eleven, and capable beyond his years.
The boys' main job was to manage two balky cows, well shod for
the road, but given to straying. In another ox cart, Benjamin
Whedon, a Connecticut schoolmaster, and his wife traveled west with
the Browns. "And I will say I found Mr. Whedon a verry kind and
Helpful Companion on the Road," Owen stated in an autobiographical
letter written in 1850.

After "47 of the most verry fatiguing days" the cavalcade halted
at Squire Hudson's to be greeted warmly like all newcomers. The
Browns did not tarry long, for Owen was impatient to show his wife
and children the cabin he had built for them but had not quite
finished when he was here on a preliminary trip the previous year.
He and his family had arrived "quit out of health we were out of
provisions and I had to go amidiatly to Youngstown for Flour," he
wrote.

Owen's cabin stood on the north side of what became the Aurora-
Hudson Road near the corner of the Cleveland Road. The tiny, one-
room log house lacked a door and windows and was almost lost in
the dark shadows of the splendid trees towering over it. But it
offered shelter of a sort and was a home in the wilderness. Owen
was confronted with the grueling task of clearing the dooryard as
quickly as possible of the trees and making his cabin weather-safe.
Opposite the cabin, across Cleveland Road, he soon built his tannery
on swift-flowing Brandywine Creek, since then ignominiously
secreted in a culvert.

The little boy who was to have so controversial a role in history fifty years later, tagged after his father everywhere, watching as he hammered up the new house, as he planted his vats and began  curing his skins. A close and lifelong father-son relationship developed.

Owen never forgot that in their first days in Hudson when they were very low on food, "the Indians brought us venson Turkey Fish and the like." He found they "were more numerous than the white People but were verry friendly, and I beleave were a benefit rather than injery there were some Persons that seamed disposed to quarel with the Indians but I never had."

Later, if hungry Indians came to Owen's door, they went away with generous gifts of bread and meal. During a tribal war in 1806 Owen, enlisting some other settlers, "went with teams and chopped drew and carried logs and put up a log house in one day a shelter for their women and children for which they appeared gratful. they were our neighbors until 1812 when the war commenced with the British [and] the Indians left these parts mostly, and rather against my wishes." It was the same sympathetic attitude that a few years hence Owen Brown and his son John were to show as champions of that other minority group, the slaves.

Following his father's example, John made friends with the Indians, wandering off to their camps, spending hours with them, fascinated by their strange ways. An Indian boy became his playmate and gave him a yellow marble which he prized—maybe his first toy. But he lost it, and was inconsolable. He never forgot the hurt.

There were other childish heartaches. A squirrel whose tail had been cut off when John trapped it became a much-loved pet—although it bit him! But it, too, disappeared, and the little boy "for a year or two looked at all the squirrels I encountered trying to discover Bobtail," he reminisced in a letter years later. A pet lamb his father had given him "sickened and died when two thirds grown." Looking back on these tragedies, he viewed them as "a much needed course of discipline on the part of the Heavenly Father."

John and his sister Anna Ruth were enrolled in the school that was only a short walk from their cabin. The Browns' friend Benjamin Whedon alternated with George Pease as teacher. The children probably found the backless benches just as uncomfortable on weekdays as on the Sabbath when the schoolhouse became a church and they were forced to sit very still during interminable sermons and wordy prayers.

Another pupil was Leonard Bacon, about John's age. During a debate scheduled one day as a school exercise, Leonard, impersonating William Penn, pleaded for kinder treatment of the Indians. John, in the role of Cortez was forced, against his nature probably, to argue for harsher treatment of the tribes.

Having been devout Congregationalists in Connecticut, the Browns joined Hudson's little church. Their modest home across the green became a natural stopping place for "the Missionaries of the Gospel . . . traviling through the Cuntry," Owen noted. He welcomed the opportunity to meet these men so much better educated than he. For all his poor spelling, Owen had a keen mind and venerated learning. Discussion during such sessions was sure to cling to the current preoccupation with Sin, Hell's awful threat, and pursuit of the grim Calvinists' elusive Salvation. At these pious gatherings hymns invariably were sung—Ruth leaving her spinning to join in.

Both she and her husband had good voices. And when singing or praying, Owen was free from the terrible stuttering that otherwise plagued him.

Owen soon was tasting some success. He was well thought of in his adopted community and was often called upon to settle complicated land disputes, frequently forced to travel considerable distances to do so. He was made an official of the church and chief fence viewer for the township. An expert tanner, his leather was selling well. He could process all kinds of native animal hides the settlers brought to him. No one could turn out a softer, sturdier piece of buckskin so much in demand, nor excel him as a shoemaker.

In 1807 he rejoiced in the birth of "another fine son," Frederick. With the first arduous years of homesteading behind him, he could write later of this time as "a period of health, peace and prosperity [that] was beginning" for him. He was "taking satisfaction, too in a verry pleasant and orderly Family"—until a December night in 1808. Then "all my earthly prospects appeared blasted. My Beloved Wife gave birth to an Infant Daughter that died in a few ours . . . and my wife followed a few ours after." His marriage had been "the beginning of days for me," he wrote. "If I have been respected in the World I must ascribe more to hir than to any other Person. She had been my help in troubel the law of kindness was ever on hir tung."

Completely demoralized, Owen stumbled through the snow to Squire Hudson's. Hudson had difficulty understanding his agitated caller, so tangled were his words with stuttering . . . He needed a grave plot . . . and there was no cemetery in the settlement . . . what was he to do. . . . The squire recalled that Benjamin Whedon had talked of deeding some of his land for burial ground. Consulted, Whedon at once offered his friend a grave site in a stretch of open land that he owned to the north of Owen's log cabin. Before long Ruth Brown's lonely resting place was marked by a tall tombstone incised with her husband's tribute, blurred today and undecipherable, but which read:

> Sacred to the Memory
> of Ruth, wife of Owen Brown
> Who died Dec. 9, 1808 in the
> 37th year of her age
> A DUTIFUL CHILD
> A SPRIGHTLY YOUTH
> A LOVING WIFE
> A TENDER PARENT
> A KIND NEIGHBOR
> And an Exemplary Christian
> "Sweet is the Memory of the Just"

Although there is no mention of the baby daughter on the gravestone or in the town records, it is safe to assume that she lies with her mother as was the custom at that time.

Owen planted a pine tree at the lonely grave—to be company for his wife. Keeping its vigil year after year, it grew tall and vigorous, annually producing a rich crop of cones that scattered over the burial place. Half a century later, after the event at Harpers Ferry, when the tree was old, people came to the cemetery to gather these cones, to cherish them and to ship them to far places in memory of Ruth's son, the Abolitionist.

For some time Ruth lay alone under her tombstone, and the pine tree kept its vigil. In 1814 Whedon sold this piece of land covering forty-two rods to the township for a cemetery. And soon other dead joined Ruth. The burial ground was further enlarged in 1828. That year the first death occurred among students at Western Reserve

College. In the days of slow transportation and little embalming, bodies could not be moved any great distance. To meet the emergency David Hudson contributed land not far from Ruth Brown's grave as a college burial plot. Later other students and college officials were interred here.

The old Hudson Township burying ground.

The college graveyard was part of the squire's apple orchard. Frugally, he stipulated that during his lifetime the apple trees were to be left standing and he was to have their fruit. The next year he assigned adjoining land for additional cemetery purposes, in return for which he was given like acreage elsewhere in the township. The Hudson Burial Ground later had an entrance on Chapel Street when that thoroughfare was laid out.

With his wife's death, Owen's world was in chaos. Ten-year-old daughter Ruth, although well trained by her mother as home helper, was overwhelmed. She was trying to take care of four brothers as well as Levi Blakeslee who was four years older than Ruth, and of Baby Frederick who cried continuously. Word of the Browns' tragedy spread quickly—the frontier had no need of telephones. Warmhearted offers of help came from Owen's neighbors, and the youngest of the Browns were parcelled out for temporary mothering in various homes.

Owen missed his lively brood. "I wanted to keep my children around me." The next year "I was unite by marrage to Sally Root a Woman of good moral character, of good intellect and well educated both in ciance and Housekeeping. I even fealt as though I could thank God that he has given me so good a substitute for the wife of youth I did not form any connection without some very searious reflections."

His new wife was one of five daughters of the highly respected Jeremiah Root family of Aurora. She was twenty. Courageously she faced the task of setting to rights a disorganized household and winning acceptance by another woman's children.

From the first, John resented her in his mother's place and became a sullen, difficult little boy. Writing almost fifty years later, he described the death of his mother as "a complete and permanent loss." Although admitting his stepmother was "a sensible, intelligent and in many ways an estimable woman," he "never adopted her in feeling."

Christian Cackler in reminiscences many years later recounted how John, abetted by his brother Salmon and by Levi Blakeslee, made Sally's life miserable, playing tricks on her that sometimes resulted in her bodily harm. Cackler had worked at Owen's tannery where

John also worked. He hated John and his comments therefore cannot be wholly depended upon. But it is clear the boy had no love for his stepmother. Whatever childish pranks he perpetrated were soon given up. When John was twelve, war was in the making, and the boy was to learn a great deal about it.

The tombstones of Sally, Owen, and Ruth Brown in the old burial ground.
Photograph by Helen Strong.

THE COMING OF
THE ELLSWORTHS

ELISHA ELLSWORTH WAS twenty-five and homesick. He missed his girl wife, Harriet (often called Harriet Elizabeth), and their baby, also named Harriet. He had left them back in Connecticut with his wife's parents, the Benjamin Oviatts. This was to be a brief stopover in Hudson. Ellsworth's father-in-law was one of the three who had bought into the township a few years before, acquiring a small part of it and the status of proprietor along with David Hudson and the Nortons.

Elisha was on the way to New Orleans to market a consignment of Goshen cheese, including the famous pineapple-shaped variety that Birdsey Norton was promoting. Young Ellsworth was one of the merchants taking advantage of the opening of the port of New Orleans to American shipping as a result of the Louisiana Purchase

maneuvered by President Jefferson in 1804. By treaty with France—
Napoleon, who had acquired that land from Spain, now needed the
money—the United States paid $15 million for over 800,000 square
miles of territory reaching from the Mississippi to the Rocky
Mountains. Considered a tremendous sum at the time, the payment
was a bargain as it practically doubled the area of the United States.
Of immediate consequence was the fact that the important port, long
closed to American commerce, was open.

Ohio, too, was entering a new period of prosperity. The year before
the purchase it had become a state, despite the opposition of
Governor St. Clair who thought the settlers not mature enough for
self-government. Ohio was the first state carved from the Northwest
Territory.

A warm welcome awaited Elisha from the many Oviatts in Hudson.
Among them was his wife's sister, Huldah, who was visiting there.
Elisha stayed most of the time at the home of his brother-in-law,
Heman Oviatt, who with his brother Benjamin Oviatt, Jr. owned
hundreds of choice Hudson acres, most of it from their father's hold-
ings.

Young Ellsworth poured out his loneliness in letters to "my beloved
wife" which happily have been preserved and give us a firsthand
glimpse of Hudson in this period, the year 1810. Life was rugged,
but perhaps less so than in most frontier settlements.

Heman Oviatt's wife, Eunice, an outstanding personality by all
accounts in the early annals, won Elisha's admiration. "She does as
much work as any woman in Hudson," he wrote to his wife. "The
plight of the Indians gained her sympathy and they count on her
as their friend. She helps her husband in his store and responds to
everyone who needs her." Some weeks before Elisha's arrival, Eunice
had nursed Huldah "through a violent turn of the Spotted Fever

when she did but just miss the Scythe of Death." Eunice had been very kind to him, too, when he "was so bad the doctor [Moses Thompson, doubtless] advised me to take a puke which I thought was very rough."

In another letter: "Attended Meeting Sunday. Heard three excellent sermons, one in the morning, the other in the afternoon [doubtless at the log church on the green], and one in the evening at Esquire Hudson's. The next day," Elisha continued, "a dozen or so of the Oviatts crowded into the Hudson house for the matrimonials of Huldah and Mr. Ira Hudson, son of the Squire. It was a hurried up affair," which, he indicated, "shocked the whole town. But it was hurried not for the reason you think but because Huldah and Ira were married without waiting for the letter from the church [written consent from the church after successive weekly readings of the bans]. Seeing that it was the intention of marriage between them, Heman Oviatt and Squire Hudson advised the step. They would rather have Priest Darrow the Missionary Preacher, then stopping briefly in the Village, should marry them than any of the Justices of the Peace, they being not very creditable men."

He added that he had learned that "Mr. Ira Hudson had been with Huldah all through her sickness and was very kind and seemed to be uncommonly affected by her illness. . . . Esquire Hudson says he will write Benjamin. . . . He hopes Harriet and her Father will not be too much upset at the news."

It was Ira who as a boy of eleven had accompanied his father on that perilous first trip to Ohio to claim the township. Elisha was favorably impressed with him, an opinion borne out, for Ira was much respected in the community.

Ira was building a house, Elisha wrote Harriet. "Huldah has left Heman's and has gone to her Father Hudson's to work at quilting

and the like till she is ready to move into their house. But it is very inconvenient for her to do her work here [at the Hudson house] there being so much company all the time."

Early in December Elisha was preparing to start on the journey to New Orleans. Storms had held up his boats on the Ohio River where freight "costs would come to $200–$300 and the distance only 80 miles." The long trip to New Orleans—five hundred miles—"will be very expensive and will add to the distance between us . . . a very tedious tour," he added, "in an open boat."

He was increasingly dejected at the separation from his family. "I know as I start south we will be farther apart before we are nearer." Yet one feels that Elisha with typical Ellsworth flair for new experiences was not averse to the trip and its adventure possibilities.

All the while he had been looking over the Hudson countryside, pressed to settle there by his Oviatt in-laws, particularly by Huldah. "She says," he told Harriet, "if you were here she would hold a day of rejoicing," and he adds, "I would make it two days." Finally, seeming to capitulate, he wrote: "I am very pleased with Heman's situation and the Country, and wish there might be some way provided for us to own a farm in this place."

He longed to see his wife and baby before going South. "It has been so long since I left my baby," he complained. In one letter he affixed a postscript: "Please remember my love to Miss Harriet, my only child and Daughter." A few years later Elisha brought his two Harriets and a small son, Augustus, to Hudson. He bought a large tract on the Cleveland-Hudson road and put up a log cabin. Eventually sons and daughters, grandchildren, and other Ellsworth relatives selected farms around him so that the road often was dubbed "the Ellsworth Road."

Elisha's twin brother, Elijah, came with them, settling in Richfield and dying at an early age. For Elisha's wife, like all women of the era with small children to care for on the road, traveling pioneer style was no easy jaunt. But for her there was the happy prospect of reunion with her sister and all the other Oviatts. Besides, Harriet was of sturdy frontier stock. She had been reared on tales of an ordeal suffered by her mother, the former Mary Carter. When a child of nine Mary had survived the bloody Indian massacre of her entire family, and had endured an exhausting trek, prodded by her captors, from her home in Delaware to Niagara Falls. There she was ransomed by the British.

Elisha for a period served as a United States custom official, attracted no doubt by the promise of exciting exploits in the revenue service. Caught one time in a savage winter storm while pursuing smugglers across ice-clogged Lake Erie, he sent his crew below to save them from freezing to death, and took the wheel himself. Ordering a keg of molasses rolled forward from a shipment on board, he stood in the sweet stuff, hoping thus to protect his legs from the zero cold. Expert though he was, his quarry eluded his cutter. Collapsing as he turned back to port, he was pulled out of the sticky mess, alas, with a badly frozen leg. The frequent frontier remedy, amputation, was resorted to. He lived many years after the experience, carrying on a very successful business from a wheelchair.

RES. OF WILLIAM W. ELLSW

HUDSON, SUMMIT CO. OHIO.

Commodore Perry's Victory on Lake Erie by John Warner Barber.

THE WAR OF 1812

A HARD-RIDING, EXCITED courier galloped into Cleveland on June 28, 1812, bringing word that a second war with Great Britain had been declared ten days before. The next day the news reached Hudson. Both towns were thrown into a frenzy of apprehension.

For sometime there had been mounting concern throughout the Western Reserve about the unsettled Indian frontier to the west of Ohio, and the suspected incitement of the tribes by the British in the Canadian area around Detroit. These issues were of greater concern to Cleveland and Hudson settlers than the impressment of American sailors by British ships, violation of United States territorial waters, blockade of American ports, and like formal grounds for war listed by President James Madison.

A Committee of Public Safety was organized immediately in Cleveland, which became headquarters for a quickly assembled militia under Generals Simon Perkins of Warren and Elisha Wadsworth of Canfield, both Revolutionary War veterans and influential in the Reserve where they owned vast tracts of land.

The Ohio Militia Roster shows that seventy-eight men from Hudson and surrounding towns volunteered, among them David Hudson's son Milo. They reported to Amos Lusk, captain, and to George Darrow, major, both of Hudson. Military drill immediately was scheduled on the green, a reassuring occurrence in itself.

In Hudson Owen Brown was soon involved. Sometime before, with his prospering business requiring a larger tannery, he had bought extensive acreage north of the village. Along with his tanning operations there he raised fine cattle, sheep, and horses. He soon was driving consignments of these animals to the United States military forces at Detroit. His son John often accompanied him.

One time the boy, then twelve years old, went alone with the herds. Keeping guard over his unruly charges, he spent most nights in the open, apparently unafraid although the route lay through what was generally considered hostile Indian territory.

More fortunate one night, John was invited to the home "of a very gentlemanly landlord," he stated many years later in writing to his young friend, Henry Stearns. The man welcomed John cordially, praising him for his courage and management of his cattle. On the other hand the man constantly berated a slave boy who waited on their supper table, at one point whipping the boy for some trifling offence. The boy was one of the slaves occasionally encountered in the area despite the Ordinance of 1787 outlawing slavery in the Northwest Territory.

Later the two boys had an opportunity to talk together out of earshot of the master. John was deeply moved by the black boy's plight and his helplessness. Recounting the incident years later when he was in his fifties, John stated that the experience made him an abolitionist then and there and led him "to declare eternal war with slavery." The sentiment was more likely that of a man in his fifties than of a young boy. Undoubtedly, however, the experience made a profound impression on John.

When Owen made the trip with John, they took the animals directly to General William Hull's encampment at Detroit. They mixed freely with the soldiers who made a pet of the tall, quiet boy. The Browns heard a great deal of camp gossip about plans for a march into Canada. They became acquainted with General Hull and admired him but were distrustful of some of the officers under him. Once back home Owen Brown could bring firsthand news to Hudson from what he sensed was an uneasy front, foreboding trouble.

Whatever misgivings he may have had were verified in mid-August. A horseman hitched his lathered mount to the white fence in David Hudson's dooryard and hurriedly sought out the squire. He brought news from officials in Cleveland: General Hull had surrendered! The British and Indians were floating down the lake in flatboats and would probably overrun this part of Ohio. Cleveland military men urged that arrangements be made at once for the safety of women and children. The authorities advised that those who could, should flee to Pittsburgh.

All Hudson was aroused. But no one left. Captain Lusk called up his men and ordered them to the green where they paraded under full arms, ready to act at the first signal. A few days later another messenger rode into town: there was no immediate danger. The boats, they had learned, carried Hull's men on parole—or, according to some, his soldiers departing A.W.O.L.

Hull's collapse left the British in command of Lake Erie. Northern Ohio consequently was open to attack. Major Darrow and the Hudson outfit were ordered to the western part of the state. Captain Lusk's men were first sent to Old Portage under command of General Wadsworth and later to Sandusky.

OLIVER H. PERRY

The situation changed dramatically in September 1813 when Comander Oliver Perry of the American Navy defeated the British fleet at Put-in-Bay in Lake Erie. For citizens of the Western Reserve, especially those in the northern section, the backbone of the war was broken. Peace did not come for nearly two years, but the fighting had moved away from Ohio to Canada.

Anticipating that once the threat of war ended, travel in the Reserve would pick up, David Hudson decided to open his house as a tavern and he applied early for a license for dispensing liquor. To make a direct route to his house he cut a road from the turn in the Aurora-Hudson Road straight west through his land over what became College Street and on over more of his property to his house. He called it Hudson Street.

There were few inns in the area at the time and Squire Hudson's was soon well patronized. His daughter Anner often presided as barmaid. When extra patrons were expected the whole family was pressed into helping prepare quantities of corn pone and other popular dishes.

By 1814 it appeared it would be safe for Anna Hudson to travel to Goshen to visit her mother. The squire thought the trip would benefit his wife who had not been well. He wrote to her en route: "My dear Wife, I have information from Buffalo that leads me to conclude you have passed the din of war"—in other words, that she was having no problems. But when she returned her health had not improved, and she died August 31, 1816. She had given birth to nine children, the youngest, David junior, was eleven. One child had died in infancy. Anna had originally made the perilous journey to Hudson by the lake route in 1800 when she was pregnant and with six children to care for.

Early in November 1816, David Hudson made the preliminary application for a license to marry Mary Robinson, the final license issued later and the wedding taking place January 1, 1817.

As Squire Hudson foresaw, with no threat of war west-going caravans again began to take to the road, and soon became more numerous than before. In the spring of 1814 Chauncey Case with his wife, Cleopatra, who was six months pregnant, and their five children drove in from Granby, Connecticut. They came in a two-horse covered wagon with a cow hitched on behind. They and their numerous descendants were to play prominent roles in Hudson's history from that day to this.

The Cases stopped first at Zina Post's on the Cleveland-Pittsburgh Road. They had known Post in Connecticut. He had settled first in Cleveland, but he and his family suffered from the miasma in the area, and he traded that property for an extensive acreage in Hudson. In 1814 he was soon to open an inn in part of his sturdy log house. He was a prominent citizen and had been one of the first to enlist during the war scare in Hudson two years before. How good it must have seemed to the Cases to climb down from their high wagon, stretch their cramped legs, and be welcomed in the strange land by an old friend!

Chauncey Case's lot (160 acres) lay four miles to the south. David Hudson had the shell of a log cabin ready for them. The fact that the cabin had only walls and a roof did not in the least dismay the Cases, according to the lively reminiscences of their son Lora. A blanket did duty for a door. For windows holes were bored through logs which could "slide back and forth under cleats." Lora described proudly how his father built an eight-foot long "fireplace of cobble-head stones laid up with clay mortar." Local clay combined with sticks made the chimney and clay was daubed in the chinks be-tween the logs. The house was completed just in time to welcome the new baby, Edward. There were to be four more.

Money was scarce, but not food. Chauncey, an expert hunter, had no need to go beyond his own woods to bring in all manner of meat for his big family, hearty fare like bear or raccoon to be roasted or, for a more delicate menu, quail and partridge snared by wheat and trapped in a net. The birds were "made into broth with dumplings" by Cleopatra.

The ingenious Chauncey, fashioning bricks from the clay at hand, built a big oven heated "by nice dry wood burnt to an ash inside it." After removing this with broom and shovel, Mrs. Case tested the temperature with her bare arm. If she could hold it in the oven until she counted twenty, it was ready for her bread. The children ate from trenchers and wooden bowls carved out by their father. Their parents used a set of pewter dishes, cherished relics of the Connecticut home.

Lora's uncle, Gideon Case, and his large family arrived, settling to the north of Chauncey's farm. Soon a room to serve as a school was added to Gideon's log house. When Lora was six he was sent to this school. Joseph and George Darrow's children also attended. All the families had large numbers of children, making a sizeable enrollment. Miss Lydia Rice was the teacher. Like all schools of the period, a main purpose was to enable the children to read the Bible. Children indoctrinated early in Calvinism chanted "In Adam's Fall, We sinned all." The curriculum was up-to-date enough to include Noah Webster's new speller. Bunyan's *Pilgrim's Progress* was often used in these early schools, the children enjoying the narrative, probably skipping over the moralizing. The teacher in those days had to have good penmanship and the pupils generally wrote legibly. Discipline was a strict no-nonsense variety, enforced by a good birch switch. But it is pleasant to think the severe prodding of New England schools lost something of its severity in the New West.

From flax grown in their own fields and wool from their sheep Lora's sisters spun while he quilled (wound thread on a bobbin) and "my mother wove. She made linen cloth bleached white for our Sunday shirts and woolen cloth for coats for all of us."

To care for the babies that followed each other in quick succession, Chauncey fashioned a large triple cradle big enough for three of the littlest children to sit in and rock the current baby, an efficient arrangement for keeping four small youngsters out of the way of their hard-working mother.

The Cases lived four miles from Hudson but were faithful attenders at the little log church on the green. In winter they traveled by sled with a tin box of hot coals brought along as a foot warmer for the women.

With a growing membership the little church could afford a full-time pastor. In 1815 the Reverend William Hanford, who had graduated from Yale University two years before, was engaged. A lot, number 56, had been set aside "for the maintenance of a regular minister of the Calvinistic Congregational faith." The new minister was to have this land. A little log house, said to have been provided by David Hudson, served as the parsonage. It was described as "a snug little cabin with a good cool cellar." Like many preachers of that day the Reverend Mr. Hanford, to augment his salary, farmed the land raising food for his family.

The women of the church, wishing to make the meagerly furnished cabin more comfortable for their pastor, invaded the parsonage one day when he was away on a missionary errand. They lined the walls with newspapers, scarce and precious items in those days. A rug and table cover of their own weaving were added, and a brass candlestick substituted for the iron holder. Hanford, coming in as his parishioners were finishing their work, exclaimed with delight: "All of this, and Heaven, too!"

He was as successful a husbandman of his fruits and vegetables as of souls, and his "cool cellar" was well stocked with products of his labor. One night, going down with a china pitcher to draw off some of his excellent cider, he stumbled and fell headlong down the stairs. The story, vouchsafed for by Lora Case, went the rounds of the village that his wife—he had married "an estimable woman" but she was less popular than her husband—hearing the clatter, rushed to the top of the stairs. "Oh, Mr. Hanford, Mr. Hanford," she cried. "Did you break my lovely pitcher?" Whereupon the preacher, smarting from his bruises, is said to have retorted angrily, "No, but by ———, I will!" and dashed the pitcher to the floor, smashing it into pieces.

John Brown, who had joined the church in 1816, taught Sabbath School. One of his pupils was Lora Case, five years his junior. The younger boy, developing what became a lifelong admiration for the sober John, kept informed of him through the tempestuous episode that marked his career. In 1859 when John Brown was in Charles Town jail awaiting execution for his Harpers Ferry assault, Case wrote him with much sympathy, offering to take the youngest Brown daughter into his family to rear her with his own girl of the same age.

Brown's reply was the last letter he wrote. He had finished his personal business, had sent off his final messages to his family, and was sitting quietly in his cell, ready for the scaffold. On learning he had another hour to live, he "calmly sat down and with the most complete composure" answered his former Sabbath School pupil. The letter, prized by Case and his family, years later was exhibited several times in the Hudson Library, and is now in the Berg Collection of the New York Public Library.

Charlestown, Jefferson, Co Va, 2, Dec, 1859.

Lora Case Esqr

My Dear Sir

Your Most Kind & cheering letter of the 28th Nov is received Such an outburst of warm hearted Sympathy not only for my self; but also for those who "have no help" compells me to steal a moment from those allowed me; in which to prepare for my last great change to send you a few words Such a feeling as you manifest makes you to "shine (in my estimation in the midst of this wicked; & perverse generation" as a light in the world" May you ever prove your self equal to the high estimate I have placed on you. Pure & undefiled religion befor God & the Father is" as I understand it: an active (not a dormant) principle— I do not undertake to direct any more about my Children. I leave that now intirely to their excellent Mother from whom I have just parted". I send you my "salu -tation with my own hand". Remember me to all yours & my dear friends. Your Friend

John Brown

I received this letter of John Brown Dec 10th 1859. Written on the day of execution

Lora Case Born Nov 18th 1811.

A FINE NEW CHURCH

AS HUDSON'S POPULATION grew so did membership in the Calvinistic Congregational Church. Clearly the village had outgrown the little log church on the green. A small group of citizens, affiliates of denominations less rigid in doctrine, had formed the Union Church, which they hoped would become a community church on ecumenical lines. In 1817 they put up a small frame building on the west side of Main Street. This church was regarded as practically an act of apostasy by most of the townspeople. It was shortlived and little data about it survives.

The little church's presence in their midst may have nudged the Congregationalists to action: it was becoming clear to them a new edifice was called for. The lot where the Village Hall now stands was selected as the site. Heman Oviatt owned the land and it was hoped he would donate it, especially as he was a deacon of the church, the second so honored after David Hudson. Oviatt, however, felt differently, explaining he already had subscribed generously to the building fund.

After a two-year impasse over the issue David Hudson and Owen Brown called on him, and by each paying him five dollars secured the deed to the property. Oviatt stipulated that timber, long cut for the proposed church and piled beside his store on Main Street must be removed before midnight of a specified day. Dr. Moses Thompson, generally considered "an infidel," managed with the help of his son to get the lumber to the church site just within the appointed hour.

The doctor, whether an unbeliever or not, seems to have been on the building committee and wanted the church to have a belfry. Accordingly he loaded his wagon with cheese, in which he dealt extensively along with his physician's duties, and drove to

Pittsburgh. There he exchanged the cheese for a bell with a pleasant tone in the key of B. When the church building was demolished more than forty years later, the bell was sold for $1,000 to a church in Independence, Ohio. As the church was going up there were numerous gifts in kind by Hudson citizens. Among the most helpful were long strings of flax spun by Cleopatra Case and used by the builders in taking measurements.

DR. MOSES THOMPSON

It was said to be the first church in the Western Reserve to have a bell and it was altogether a challenging project. It was completed in 1820, the cost $5,400 representing a great deal of money for that day. At the dedication the debt was wholly cleared by income from the pews, or slips as they were called. If the Goshen plan was followed, these slips were assigned to a member according to his official position in the village or the amount of property he had. The aged if hard of hearing were given seats well in front. Wives sat across the aisle with the children so that they could be kept in order during the long service.

In a contemporary reference to the church the Reverend Stephen Bradstreet of Cleveland described it as having "immense fluted columns supporting the roof, circular pews in the middle of the House and square old pews around the sides." He added, "It seemed to me as severe and uncomfortable a place of worship as the grimmest old Puritan could devise." The floor and pews were bare and there was no heat even in the most severe weather. In winter women provided themselves with tin boxes filled with coals from the home hearth, but their menfolk sat out the long sessions stoically enduring the cold.

Sunday, which began at sundown Saturday, was a day to be lived through somehow. Talking was curbed with only necessary conversation allowed, even for children. They in turn were forbidden to play or to engage in the simplest games. The only reading permitted was the Bible or other acceptable works like *The Book of Martyrs* by the sixteenth-century dour English theologian John Foxe. All meals were of cold food for there was no cooking on the Sabbath. In such a regime the two-hour morning and afternoon sermons—a preacher was shortchanging his congregation if he talked less—were welcome diversions.

Hudson's Calvinistic Congregational Church was the bastion of morality and pointed the way to salvation. Church membership was not taken lightly. To be admitted to membership required personal appearance before the entire congregation followed by a prayerful meeting of the deacons to pass on the applicant. To bolster righteousness in the home members, a visiting committee went about two-by-two calling on families, counseled them and prayed with them to insure that they showed concern for their souls' well-being in the everlasting hereafter. The men selected for these duties were: Owen Brown and Heman Oviatt as one pair; George Kilbourne and Gideon Mills another; and Gideon Case and Benjamin Whedon. Deacon Hudson was a visitor at large.

Special meetings were held to hear evidence presented against members accused of conduct unbecoming to a Christian. Samuel Bishop for one "had behaved in a disorderly manner in the home of Heman Oviatt," it was asserted. Another time he had fought with Christian Cackler, seizing him by the throat. He had called someone else "a damned dirty pup." Refusing to come before the elders in person, Bishop sent a letter "notifying the church I do withdraw from this communion, and I pray God may forgive you." The church meeting adjourned in sorrow but with the hope the "offender would exhibit marks of repentance."

Benjamin Oviatt on one occasion was charged with language bordering on profanity, of disturbing the peace, and of disrupting family worship. He admitted his wrongdoing in writing, and his "confession was accepted as satisfactory."

The church also functioned in a marriage counseling role. It was not unusual for a husband and wife, caught up in a domestic problem, to come before the body as a couple and air their troubles. Stephen Thompson junior presented himself voluntarily to declare that in a dispute with his wife he "was at fault, using strong language without provocation and badly frightening her." He professed repentance and shame, "asked forgiveness of God . . . and of his brethren and sisters." He was prayed over, and his standing in the church reestablished. Word reached the church fathers that all was not well between Brother Gideon Mills and his wife. David Hudson and Owen Brown were appointed a special committee to labor with them. Brother Mills shortly came before the congregation to assume the blame. It was decided that if he would sign a confession and read it publicly, "the church would be satisfied."

Everyone knew everyone else and tales of their neighbors' peccadilloes without a doubt provided plenty of diverting gossip. After all it was a time of lean entertainment fare when even a newspaper was treasured. So it happened that every household was atwitter with the startling news that the highly respected Deacon Whedon had been caught in the net. Ever since his arrival with his friend Owen Brown he had been looked up to as a churchman and civic leader.

The charge against him, presented in writing, stated that he had opened his house to a puppet show, "the exhibit of which [as everybody knew] is recognized by the church as an immoral practice." The house, built a few years before on the south side of Aurora Street not far from the green, was—and remains—one of the handsome early homes of the village.

Whedon apparently ignored the accusation and was indifferent to the committee assigned to examine him, although it was headed by David Hudson. In fact Whedon compounded his offence a few weeks later by "admitting fiddlers and letting his house be occupied for Balls and dances." "This," it was pointed out, "was inconsistent with the duties of a Christian and in violation of the solemn convenant that he and other members of the church entered into years ago." Who, one wonders, attended such evil programs and why were they not censured as well as the deacon?

The talk in town was that his wife, although aware of the church attitude, staged the ball—and maybe the puppet show, too—without her husband's knowledge. The deacon, however, did not use his wife's behavior as an excuse—no hiding behind petticoats for him. He simply made no reply. The committee held many prayer sessions over Brother Whedon, hoping for a sign of repentance from him. When none came at the end of six months, he was excommunicated and a public notice of the fact posted on the door of the church the following Sunday.

The church served the community until 1865 when the brick church with the soaring steeple was built on Aurora Street near College Street. It cost $10,000 and was dedicated debt free just forty-five years to the day after dedication of the first church. Architect of the new edifice was Simeon Porter, formerly of Hudson, who at that time had his office in Cleveland. He was the son of Lemuel Porter

who had been in charge of the first building on the campus of Western Reserve College.

Since its founding the church had operated under the double name of the First Congregational Church of Hudson and the First Congregational Calvinistic Society of Hudson. At the annual meeting of the parish in 1957, a historic event took place: church members voted to change the name to the First Congregational Church of Hudson. The move eliminated the double name under which the church had functioned for 140 years. It also reflected the long-standing general rejection of the stern tenets of Calvinism for the gentler theology of the modern era.

House built by John Brown on Hines Hill Road.

DIANTHE

EIGHTEEN-YEAR-OLD John Brown made up his mind to become a minister of the gospel, and decided to train at the Plainfield Academy in Massachusetts. His father, Owen, feeling there was no higher calling for man than the pulpit, endorsed his son's idea, giving him one of his best horses for the journey.

To his consternation John found the school nothing like what he had expected. The stalwart youth, five feet, ten inches tall, was a man beside the boys who were his classmates. They were not only conspicuously better attired than he but, to his humiliation, much better prepared, handling with ease such assignments as those in Latin and Greek that meant nothing to the big man-boy from the West. He pored over his lessons well into the night until his candle burned out and his eyes smarted, but he made no headway. He transferred to Morris Academy with no more success there. Discouraged, he gave up and headed for home where he took up surveying. He never referred to his abortive effort to become a clergyman: no mention of the experience appears in his journals or letters.

JOHN BROWN

With his father's remarriage he found on his return that the family home was crowded by the inevitable succession of babies. John, joining with Levi Blakeslee, decided to set up bachelor quarters on Owen's land to the north of the village on what is now called Hines Hill. Owen had established a large tannery there and put both young men to work in it, also relying on them to look after his herds of blooded cattle pastured on the slope.

The bachelors engaged the Widow Lusk "to do" for them. She

was of aristocratic stock, tracing her lineage to the prominent Adams family. Her late husband, Amos, had died from the fever that had attacked him and many of the troops in the War of 1812. His widow's aristocratic heritage put no food on the family table and she was glad for the work in the bachelors' cabin. Sometimes she brought

along her daughter Dianthe to help especially with the bread making in which the girl was particularly adept. Her brother Milton was devoted to his sister and called her his "guardian angel." She sang beautifully, he thought, mostly hymns which he liked to listen to. There was a place in the woods he knew about where she went alone to pray. He described her as "pleasant and cheerful but plain," and declared, "She never said anything but what she meant. At home she was always ready to help and was a good cook."

Returning one evening after a long hard day in the tannery, John found the cabin filled with the delectable odor of freshly baked bread that Dianthe was taking from the hearth. She had made it, her mother volunteered. The sleeves of the young woman's linsey-woolsey dress were rolled back, revealing plump, well-formed arms, and her cheeks were attractively pink from the heat of the fire. Perhaps it was the first time John really had looked at the girl. No likeness of Dianthe exists, but John, referring to her years later, called her "remarkably plain"—again this description of her—but "she was an economical girl of good common sense."

There would have been no midnight trysts on the hill for the couple and it is difficult to imagine a kiss escaping from John's implacable, thin lips. "Prompted," however, "by my father, and my own inclination," he wrote years later, he married her when he was twenty and she a year younger, the local minister, the Reverend William Hanford, conducting the nuptials, probably in Hudson's new Congregational Church that was dedicated that year. Blakeslee left Hudson and settled in Wadsworth, Medina County where he set up a tannery. Dianthe's brother Milton, who hated John, refused to attend the ceremony. He never forgot how John had turned him away abruptly when he walked up the hill to call on his sister one Sunday. The boy at sixteen had been apprenticed to David Hudson and Sunday was the only free day he had. John, however, with Calvinistic righteousness, countenanced no visiting on the Lord's Day. Dianthe seems to have accepted her husband's dictates: indeed few individuals dared cross his stern commands.

Influenced by his father's concern for the blacks, John welcomed runaway slaves who by some secret alchemy knew his farm was a safe stopover. Wakened in the night by a furtive knock on the cabin door, Dianthe would leave her bed to prepare food for the trembling visitors, she or John taking the meal to a hideout beside a big rock in the woods. On such errands she was as terrified in the inky darkness as the Negroes.

The first year of their marriage John junior was born, to be followed by a succession of other babies. John was proud of his children. Yet when he heard four-year-old John junior reciting a fanciful tale, he beat the boy for the sake of his salvation. Albeit the father's cheeks were wet with tears, he put all his sinewy strength into the blows. Dianthe may have comforted her sobbing son secretly but she knew it would have been useless to interfere with the punishment. John was equally inflexible with the men who worked for him, requiring them to join the family at dawn for worship every day and to attend church on Sunday. He mellowed somewhat, however, as he grew older, according to their daughter Ruth who is quoted as saying her father told her he regretted his strict handling of his children and if he "had his life to live over would do so differently."

John worked hard and prospered. He could afford to supplant the log cabin with a sturdy frame house that stands today, although much altered. A segment of the Erie Canal was pushing into the

Cuyahoga Valley a few miles away. Hudson was growing: it would seem to have been a good place for a young man to plant the roots of his future. But a chronic restlessness that was to plague John Brown the rest of his life beset him. On a surveying trip in western Pennsylvania he had come on virgin land with oak trees that would provide bark for a tannery, as well as grasslands for cattle which could be marketed not far off in Pittsburgh. He at once took title to an extensive acreage there.

Returning to Hudson in April he would have been in time for an impressive event in which his father participated: the laying of the cornerstone of Western Reserve College. But John was pulling up stakes, moving to the Pennsylvania wilderness. If Dianthe had been consulted about the move, she probably would not have raised her voice in dissent.

Fruit trees John had set out were breaking into bloom, promise of riches to come. His hillside fields lay bare to the spring sun, waiting for the plough. In the dooryard a clump of bluebells someone had given Dianthe were in bud. Around the wellhead she had set out cockleshells, treasures of her girlhood.

The Browns and their little boys were leaving it all. Dianthe with her baby in her arms crawled up on the high wagon seat beside her husband. The other two boys she settled behind her in the wagon amidst the small bundles of the Browns' few clothes. John slapped reins on the horses. They were fine horses—he never owned any other kind. The wagon creaked forward down the hill. Dianthe turned to gaze at the house—the best she would ever know—the bluebells just coming into bud and the orchard in a froth of pink.

Their new home was in a virgin forest, in an untamed section of Crawford County. They managed as best they could until John built a stout cabin. He cleared twenty-five acres and put up a tannery shed before the first frost. Difficult as he was to live with, he could not be accused of indolence. He was appointed postmaster, a shelf in the cabin designated as the post office. Dianthe handed out the few letters that came, glad of the task as it gave her someone to talk to now and then.

Three months after they had arrived at their woodland home, another child, Frederick, was born, named for one of John's brothers. When the boy was four years old he died, the first of several children they were to lose. Shortly after this tragedy, they had another son

and, as frequently happened in those days, he was given the dead child's name. Between the death and birth of the two Fredericks, Dianthe's daughter Ruth was born. She was to play a sagacious role in the tragic drama of John Brown.

When Dianthe was thirty-one and had lived six years in the bleak wilderness home, she gave birth to her seventh child, a son. The baby died at birth, his mother following him a few days later. Shrouded in her wedding dress that someone found packed in lavender leaves on a high cabin shelf, she was buried beside the baby in the lonely woodland. John sent word of his loss to his father: "We are again smarting under the rod of our Heavenly Father. Last night . . . my affectionate, dutiful and faithful Diantha (to use her own words) 'bad farewell to earth,'" he wrote. "Her health was very poor, I think I mentioned in my last letter. She, however, kept about a bit when she was brought to bed of a son (not a living one). . . . We called a good physician who was obliged to take the child with

instruments. . . . He advised her the situation was most critical, but this information did not depress her spirits. . . . 'I thought I might go to rest on God's Sabbath,' she said." At her request her children were brought to her and she with heavenly composure gave faithful advice to each.

Early biographies of John Brown suggest that Dianthe was insane at the time of her death, but John's letter puts this claim to rest: "Her reason," he wrote, "was unimpaired and her mind composed with the Peace of God. Tomorrow she is to be laid beside her dear little son." A marker amidst the weeds and grasses carried this legend:

In memory of Dianthe
wife of John Brown
She died August 10th
1832. Aged 31 years.
Farewell Earth.

JOHN BROWN

MARY ANNE BROWN

Mary Anne with daughters Anne b. 1843 and Sarah b. 1846.

MARY ANNE

WIDOWER JOHN BROWN with five children, from eleven-year-old John junior to baby Frederick, engaged a neighbor girl as housekeeper. She brought along her sister Mary Anne to help with the spinning. Their father, Charles Day, once a prosperous blacksmith, had lost his property and his daughters were glad of the work. Mary seemed older than her seventeen years. She kept the spinning wheel twirling by the hour, turning into excellent yarn the fleece John had clipped from his sheep.

John eyed her with approval. He noted that the children liked her and that she was particularly attentive to baby Frederick. She was

House where Mary Anne and John Brown were married.

not Dianthe but Mary had her own good points. He presented his proposal in writing. Sensing its message, Mary carried the envelope in her apron pocket for a couple of days. John grew impatient. Following her to the well one evening as she went to bucket up water, he demanded her answer. Mary still hesitated. The marriage would mean raising another's children and union with an awesome being nearly twice her age. There was little in such a bridegroom to inspire a seventeen year old. But Mary sensed marriage would lighten the heavy load of her parents and there were few opportunities for a young woman in the sparsely settled region.

Mary came into the cabin to assume all the housework, all the care of the five little Browns Dianthe had left. Fortunately Mary was spared foreknowledge of the tumult and tragedy that lay ahead for her, but she was staunchly made and was to survive her husband a quarter of a century.

She became the mother of thirteen children. Her first child, Sarah, was born in the spring of 1834 following her marriage, the next year her first son, Watson. He was to die twenty-four years later in his father's abortive raid at Harpers Ferry. Before Watson was a year old, his father's roaming nature once more got the best of him. He moved Mary and her two little ones along with Dianthe's five to Franklin Mills, today's Kent, Ohio, where he expected to establish a tannery. Speculative operations in a real estate venture collapsed and the general panic of 1837 struck a final blow, leading him into bankruptcy and bringing on litigation with endless creditors.

For a brief interlude he settled his family in Hudson, unfailing refuge. With his fortunes at a low ebb, his family shunted between Franklin Mills and Hudson. Mary, worried by scanty means and her husband's troubles, continued to have babies every year or two. The sensitive Oliver who was to lose his life at Harpers Ferry was born in 1839 during one of the short stops at Franklin Mills.

It was about this time that John persuaded Mary and Dianthe's oldest sons to join him in a holy pact "to do all in their power to abolish slavery." Liberation of the Negro loomed more and more prominently in John Brown's thoughts until the cause obsessed him, and in his own words became "the greatest or principal object of my life." Early he concluded the black man's chains could be broken only by armed aggression, with bloodshed unavoidable. In such a mood he committed Mary and his oldest sons to the enterprise. The convenant motivated his actions for the next twenty years, the remainder of his life, and underlay Mary's attitude and reactions.

The Browns' migrations took them to Richfield in 1842. That was near enough to Hudson to keep John in touch with his father and affairs of the village. Mary, at twenty-six, was expecting her seventh child. John was bankrupt now, stripped by law of most of his livestock: he was allowed to retain only two mares, two cows, two hogs, some sheep, and chickens. Mary and John were thus starting anew. Their first home in Richfield was a log structure. Mary had barely time to arrange their few possessions before Austin was born.

The Browns had been in Richfield a year when catastrophe struck. John was in New England, ostensibly concerned with sheep and wool, but actually developing contacts with important abolitionists; more and more the Negro cause was absorbing him. Meanwhile Mary was confronted with a houseful of very sick children: six-year-old Charles died. Neighbors procured a coffin, dug a grave in the local cemetery, and stayed with her as the small body was lowered into the ground. Three older children were ill and grew steadily worse. Peter, aged three, died, followed the next day by Mary's firstborn, Sarah, nine. Baby Austin died a week after his first birthday. Mary's neighbors helped her lay three little bodies in one coffin and placed it in a new grave beside the earlier one. A single headstone marked the children's resting place in the hillside cemetery. The children died of "black diphtheria," according to Mrs. Mason Oviatt, affectionately referred to by her neighbors as "Aunt Fannie," who was helpful throughout the ordeal.

Mary, who was pregnant again, was worn-out by nursing and grief and almost died. Her next baby, Anne, was born three months later, two days before Christmas. The birth did not interfere with any holiday celebration for John's Puritan conscience disapproved of such festivity.

The following year, 1844, Mary and her children were uprooted again. John had concluded the most auspicious business venture of his career—partnership with Colonel Simon Perkins, Jr., a wealthy Akron resident. John was to take charge of Perkins's fifteen hundred sheep pastured on the hills that soon would overlook Akron factories. Also he was to act as commission merchant of the wool produced. Best of all from Mary's point of view they were given a good house. But sorrow invaded the idyllic situation: Mary's ninth child, Amelia, born the first year at Perkins Hill, fell into a tub of wash water and was fatally scalded. John was away at this time. Two weeks after the funeral Mary had a letter from him: "This is a bitter cup, but blessed be

God. . . . I trust you will be able to bear it in some measure as you ought. I exceedingly regret that I am unable to return . . . to share your trials with you."

After two years in Akron John opened a wool headquarters for Perkins and Brown in Springfield, Massachusetts and moved his family to the eastern city. The home he selected on a "back street" in an undesirable part of town "would have satisfied a Spartan" according to Frederick Douglass. The eloquent former slave had been in touch with John since meeting him in Hudson. There was an air of plainness about the house and its furniture that to Douglass "almost suggested destitution." The Negro did not know that money had been allocated for furnishings but John, calling Mary and the children to him, put the proposition: should they spend this money for their own comfort or send it "to the poor blacks," and of course the blacks won.

The prosperous Akron interlude was brief. John was a better shepherd than merchant: wool piled up in the warehouse unsold; he involved the company in a series of disastrous deals, and breakup of the partnership was inevitable. About this time he met Gerrit Smith, a northern New York philanthropist who had inherited a primeval tract of many acres in the Adirondack country. With strong convictions as to his obligations to God and the Negro, he offered plots to "worthy colored people and escaped slaves" hoping they would clear the land and lay out farms.

John heard about Smith's plan, called on him at his home in Peterboro, New York and proposed to live among the colonizing blacks to oversee and guide them. Smith was overjoyed at the prospect of cooperation from John Brown, a farmer, a well-tried pioneer, and as devout a Christian and abolitionist as himself. He sold John and his sons Jason and Oliver two farms of over two hundred acres, at one dollar an acre. The property was near North Elba, three miles south of what later became the village of Lake Placid. The land was remote, untouched by civilization with few passable roads leading to it.

Deciding to look over the new holdings, John took Mary and the current infant, six-month-old Ellen, as far as Mary's brother's home in Whitehall, New York. Ellen contracted a cold and by the time they were back in Springfield the little girl was very ill. John, who happened to be home, walked the floor with the sick little girl and sang hymns to her. She died in his arms and her father broke down and sobbed. They were planning to go to see the home in the Adirondacks. Mary could not bear to leave Ellen's body, so it was placed temporarily in a vault and later interred in the cemetery on the Old Military Road in North Elba.

A cold spring rain was falling when John took his wife and children to view the property he had selected in the mountains. The family was piled into a sturdy wagon behind a yoke of plodding oxen, replaced later by a span of spirited horses. The available shelter, they found, was a tiny house, its main room "answering for a kitchen, dining room and parlor." The two bedrooms were equipped with four beds so that wayfarers might be accommodated. Before noon a weary young slave who had tramped all the way from Florida came to the door, to be welcomed as one of the family.

Although matters were not going well for Perkins and Brown in Akron, the partnership held for several years. John decided to market the company's wool in England. Leaving his family at North Elba, in 1849 he carried out this ill-advised junket. John found that the American wool was rejected by British buyers, and what he did sell was at ruinous prices. Back in New York he brought most of his consignment with him, unsold. Resultant losses were estimated at $40,000.

While John was away, Mary, with children of varying ages, was in charge of the North Elba farm's meager harvest as well as the blooded cattle John had imported. In addition she faced constant problems with the Negroes who settled here and for whom homesteading was not a success. Her health gave way. She betook herself to a water cure establishment in Massachusetts, leaving the household in charge of Ruth who recently had married a local farmer, Henry Thompson. It appears to be the only time that Mary indulged in care for herself.

House furnished to the John Brown family in Akron by Colonel Simon Perkins.

After John's return from his disastrous wool-selling efforts, the long-suffering, patient Perkins called him back to Akron. Mary and the children made ready for the road. Recalling the pleasant Akron house they again were to occupy, Mary was not sorry to go. A few months after they were settled, John, writing to his son John junior about the peach and apple crops, casually added that Mary "was confined by the birth of the largest and strongest boy she ever had." But the boy died before he could be named. His mother, "taken with bleeding of the lungs was in bed now and then but manages to be about a good deal and get much done." Two years later Mary's last child arrived—her thirteenth and John's twentieth. They named her Ellen in memory of the Ellen they had lost.

House erected by Henry Thompson for the Brown family in North Elba.

North Elba, never out of John Brown's mind, then beckoned them once more. In 1855 the wandering Browns set out again for the mountain home. It would be their permanent base. From this date until Mary's widowhood, the outpost in the Adirondacks was home for all of them. The house had four rooms and a dormitory loft. It was erected by Henry Thompson and was unplastered and unfinished on their arrival. Life unfolded for Mary on as primitive a scale as if this were a century earlier. The plow fought tree stumps. Winter lingered for six months. Amidst mountain grandeur the hillsides were so eroded crops scarcely could be coaxed out of the thin soil.

Transportation bogged down in bad weather. Mary got out her spinning wheel and loom, set up a cavernous iron kettle for hog butchering and rendering, tapped the maple trees for syrup, milked the cows, gave thanks when she could hang a side of beef. Her husband's herds thrived on the steep slopes that supported little else. John Brown shook off the encumbrances of the commercial world for which he was so ill-fitted and plunged zestfully into the rough life. He was at heart a pioneer.

But his chronic hunger for roaming began to goad him. Five of his sons—Dianthe's John junior, Jason, Owen, and Frederick and Mary's Salmon—were in Kansas, a territory recently opened to colonizers. John wanted to see these far-off lands. A letter from John junior reported the people were stirred to fever pitch over the Kansas-Nebraska Act. Passed in 1854 it permitted settlers to determine the slavery issue, voting the state into the Union as either slave or free. John junior wrote they needed arms to defend themselves against "scoundrels who would fasten slavery on this glorious land."

This was rhetoric the father could not resist: fresh, empty land to explore, reunion with his boys from whom he never liked to be separated, above all God's cause summoning him in the name of the downtrodden slave. Mary laid a simple meal on the table; the family and three Negro hands took their places. John fingered the letter that had come from Kansas summoning him in the name of the slave; suddenly he announced he was going to Kansas. Straight off!

For nearly four years he would give himself to his mission of keeping Kansas and adjoining territories free from slavery. He would spend his energies either maneuvering in the area or traveling about from New England to Chicago raising funds and winning supporters for freedom.

Mary seldom would be out of his thoughts. He wrote to her regularly, more often than she to him. Mary was not a letter writer. Besides, she seldom knew where to address him. John was associated with many women in promotion of his cause. But there never was so much as a hint that his interest or loyalty ever wandered to anyone but Mary, the wife he had left in their lonely northern homestead.

John departed for Kansas in August 1855. Henry Thompson and Oliver went with him. It was October before they reached John's sons' makeshift shanties at Osawatomie. The young Browns, shivering in cutting winds, were too ill to gather their crops. In their faraway citadel, Mary and Watson faced the winter that swept in early and stayed late, bringing sub-zero temperatures, piling snow in drifts that clogged the roads. The ill-built house was poor protection, a fact John seemed to realize: he wrote her "regretting the cold house," but, he reminded her, "the lot of the slave is worse."

Shattering news came to Mary, garbled versions of the Pottawatomie slaughter (May 1856): five proslavery settlers in the night were routed from their beds and into their dooryard. With no opportunity to defend themselves they were dispatched by John Brown and his sons. Though Brown subsequently attempted to dodge responsibility and vindicate the massacre, he had ordered and planned the deed whether or not he participated. The affair left an indelible stain on his name.

Salmon returned to North Elba and reported what had happened. John junior was sickened to temporary insanity. Young Oliver and Frederick turned away in revulsion, their hands clean. Salmon and Watson were digging potatoes one October day when they learned of fresh violence in Kansas. Their brother Frederick had been attacked and killed at Osawatomie. It was proslavery revenge for the Pottawatomie outrage in which, ironically, Frederick had not taken part. His brothers left their big rush basket half filled with tubers and made ready to go to at once to Kansas.

Then there was no man at North Elba. Mary was in charge, left to care for the farm and the young women and children living with her and depending on her: two Thompson women, Ruth and her sister-in-law, with their husbands in Kansas, brought their babies. The small cabin was near to bursting. Winter was coming on apace—a hard winter. Warm clothing and food for them all and fodder for the animals had to be found. From travelers stumbling on the Brown home a picture of Mary emerges: her house immaculate despite overcrowding. No conveniences. Simple food in frugal quantity. A spotless white cloth on the table. Ruth Thompson, her deputy manager, devoted to her as were all Dianthe's children. Mary reserved, overseeing everything in neat, shabby dress as gaunt as an oak ravaged by winter gales—and as unbowed.

John was on the move in "Kansas Territories" or crisscrossing the country, exhorting before antislavery conventions in New York State, in Cleveland one week, Chicago the next. There were frequent stopovers in Hudson. The village drew him back as long as his father Owen lived. John's Pottawatomie crimes, not widely known, were seldom mentioned. He was a striking figure. Stooped from hard work and a rigorous life, his beard, the lines of weariness in his face, all made him appear an old man. And he was only fifty-nine when he was hanged in 1859.

DEACON DAVID HUDSON

A view over backyard fences of South College.

WESTERN RESERVE COLLEGE

THE TERRITORIAL LEGISLATURE'S refusal in 1801 to grant a charter for a college in the Connecticut Western Reserve did not discourage David Hudson or the others behind the movement. In 1803, shortly after Ohio became a state, petitions for such a charter again were circulated, this time successfully. Forthwith the Erie Literary Society "with collegiate powers" was organized by thirteen incorporators headed by Hudson. The location of the proposed institution was the subject of long debate and many meetings.

An offer, however, by an absentee Connecticut landowner of eleven hundred acres for a campus at Burton settled the question. One can imagine the frustration of Squire Hudson who without doubt had pushed the desirability of his town for the campus. Using great foresight, as it developed, he nonetheless continued as president of the society's board, serving for more than twenty years. The position enabled him to keep in touch with all the subsequent events connected with higher education in the Reserve.

The first building of the society went up shortly on Burton's public square. Peter Hitchcock, five years out of Yale, was engaged in 1806 as principal. "Our College," as Burton citizens optimistically referred to the undertaking, got under way haltingly. Disaster struck in 1810 when a fire destroyed the main building. Nine years passed before it was replaced. The interim meant a setback for the school, its status reaching little more than an academy.

Its founders had envisioned it as a center where "pious youth" would be trained for the ministry, and also some laity, it was hoped, could be prepared as teachers, physicians, and the like. Churches were increasing so rapidly in the Reserve that there were not enough qualified men to fill the pulpits and there were few trained laity. Congregational and Presbyterian clergymen were needed. The churches functioned under presbyteries. Hudson, for example, being in Portage County (Summit County was not created until 1840) was within the Portage Presbytery. The area west of the Cuyahoga River was known as the Huron Presbytery and that around Burton as the Grand River Presbytery.

Representatives from all three groups were appointed to solicit funds for a theological department at Burton. It was reasoned that the academy thus expanded would become a bona fide college. David Hudson at the moment could give little attention to this effort: he was confronted with a problem in his own town. In 1821 he discovered that Birdsey Norton Oviatt, his clerk in the post office, had been stealing money from the mails, a sum of around $600 all told, and he had him promptly arrested. Hudson was particularly upset because Oviatt was his son-in-law, his daughter Abigail Laura's husband, and a man the squire had trusted implicitly. Most of the money was recovered but the scandal rocked the community. Twenty-three-year-old Laura divorced Oviatt and came to live with her parents.

The Burton school, Hudson soon discovered, was in trouble. The feeling was growing among the trustees that the town was the wrong location for it. New highways and stagecoach routes had bypassed it. Local residents were not supporting it; many early pledges remained unfulfilled. Most telling of all, the town was considered to have an unhealthful environment with a great deal of sickness from malaria, or, in common parlance, "the shakes."

Hudson was quick to act. He made two attempts, one in 1823, the other the next year, to have the institution moved to Hudson. Both efforts were defeated. This was largely because if Burton lost the academy, the original large gift of land would revert to the donor, and the school thus would forfeit its major asset.

Before long it was determined that despite the loss of the land a new situation must be found for the contemplated college. Word of this decision was widely circulated throughout the Reserve. The three presbyteries named four commissioners as a Committee of Location. For the next eight months the committee, meeting in various parts of the Reserve, studied qualifications of the many towns hopeful of being selected for the college. One application came from General Simon Perkins of Warren who offered a large acreage at the Portage summit of the Cuyahoga River. Since no settlement was there at the time, the offer was rejected. The land now is in the center of the city of Akron.

The committee finally limited its consideration to Aurora, Tallmadge, Euclid, Cleveland, and Hudson. Aurora was soon eliminated because of a malaria-breeding swamp. Euclid was not centrally located, and Tallmadge, it was claimed, was not giving sufficient support to the academy it already had. Cleveland, then a town of seven hundred, was seriously considered, and offered many advantages. But it was a lake port, and this meant the presence of sailors, who were considered a rough lot, and it was feared they would contaminate the students.

Hudson alone remained, presenting many advantages not the least of which was the personality of David Hudson. With the decision to abandon the Burton campus, Squire Hudson resigned as president of the Lake Erie Literary Society, thus feeling free to work for selection of his town as the college site. He emphasized the main highways that were routed through the town, largely, he could have said, built as a result of his leadership. From the first he had worked for improved roads, and his town was on the main road to Pittsburgh as well as the road north to Cleveland. He saw to it that the new Chillicothe Road included Hudson. It was routed south from Painesville on Lake Erie through to Aurora where it turned southwest to Hudson, thence south to the diagonal known as Hudson Road to Akron, and on to Chillicothe, seat of the capital when Ohio became a state. A stagecoach route through Hudson recently had been inaugurated.

Most telling of all, the practical squire faced the financial needs. Calling townspeople together in June 1824, he asked for pledges to underwrite the proposed college providing it was located in Hudson. Within a few months $5,000 was subscribed, a surprisingly large sum for this community at that time. David Hudson promised an additional $2,142, indeed a generous gift. The Presbyteries' Education Committee had collected $3,000. Thus more than $10,000 was in sight, the amount considered ample for starting the institution.

The final meeting to settle on the location took place in Euclid in January 1825. The village of Hudson was chosen. The energetic commissioners mounted their horses and galloped off to proclaim their decision to the lucky hamlet.

Two areas in Hudson were selected by the citizens as desirable for the campus, one in a southern part of the village, its exact location now uncertain. The other, which the committee preferred, was in the northeastern section on a ridge. Here the officials bought 6.7 acres from the estate of the late Gideon Case, paying $42.00 an acre, then considered a high price. With these formalities concluded, committee members headed their horses up the hill to the property. One of them dismounted and in a dramatic gesture pounded a stout stake into the frozen ground proclaiming, "This is the College Plot." Shortly a second parcel of 3.77 acres, immediately to the north of the first and extending to Hudson Street was purchased from David Hudson. These two plots made the original campus. It is frequently stated that this first campus was donated by Squire Hudson. He did make a gift of one hundred and sixty acres at this time, but it was in a swampy area in another part of the township. It was sold by the college at a later date for three dollars an acre. His contribution of the substantial sum of money plus his organizing of financial support by the townspeople were the motivating forces that made the college possible. He was indeed the founder of Western Reserve College.

Twelve members of the Education Committee and four others appointed by the Huron Presbytery rode their horses through a February snowstorm in 1826 to meet in Hudson. They named themselves college trustees with the Reverend Caleb Pitkin elected president. A Yale graduate and former pastor in Charleston, Ohio, he had been active in all the preliminary organization activities.

The Ohio Stone Quarry in Peninsula circa 1860.

Benjamin Whedon was made treasurer. David Hudson, Owen Brown, and Heman Oviatt were put in charge of erecting the first building and were named trustees. Thus the new college was launched by local men and guided by the able and indefatigable Pitkin, who soon moved to Hudson. He was particularly acceptable as he had trained for the ministry under the much-loved Reverend Asahel Hooker of Goshen, Connecticut, former home of so many Hudson villagers.

While the college was coming into being, construction of the Ohio Canal a few miles from Hudson was proceeding at a feverish pace under the all-seeing direction of the tireless Alfred Kelley of Cleveland. Blocks of sandstone for the locks were quarried at nearby Peninsula and oak for the heavy sluice gates was cut in the surrounding forests. The groundbreaking at Portage Summit in the summer of 1825 marked the beginning of construction on the first part of the waterway, the section between Cleveland and Akron. Two years later, on Independence Day, this segment was formally

Drawing of a canal packet courtesy of the Western Reserve Historical Society.

opened. David Hudson and his wife, riding from Akron to Cleveland ensconced in seats of honor, participated in the thirty-six mile voyage in the first boat to make the trip. Both accomplishments—the canal and the college—were born of the same pioneer zeal and initiative.

What to name the college was a subject of much discussion. It was first called The Collegiate Institution in the Connecticut Western Reserve, and soon shortened by Pitkin to A College for the Western Reserve. On an order for lumber it was shortened accidentally to Western Reserve College, which was adopted forthwith as the name.

The trustees were scarcely organized before they were confronted with trouble. Led by representatives from the Burton area, some members of the state legislature opposed granting the college a charter. Pitkin, greatly alarmed, swung into his saddle and traveled as fast as his horse could carry him fifty miles northwest to Brownhelm in Lorain County to enlist the help of judge Henry Brown. Brown had statewide influence politically and was a college trustee appointed by the Huron Presbytery. The two men decided it was imperative that they plead their cause personally before the state officials. Accordingly, in the face of a gathering winter storm, the two turned their horses southward for the one hundred and fifty mile trip to Columbus, the state

REV. CALEB PITKIN

capital. By his prompt action, Pitkin, with the Judge Brown's adroit maneuvering, saved the issue—the coveted charter was signed in February 1826.

No time was lost in pushing building plans. The energetic building committee named Heman Oviatt as contractor, and to hurry construction set April 26 as the day for laying the cornerstone of the new building. It is to the great credit of the trustees and the everlasting good fortune of the village of Hudson that the master builder, Lemuel Porter, was selected to put up the first structure and to become what would be known today as the college architect. The previous year he had completed the impressive Congregational church in neighboring Tallmadge where he had settled a short time before. The steepled edifice was known and admired throughout the Reserve. Porter was from Waterbury, Connecticut and served on the college Committee of Location. He was a Mason and, what really assured his selection, a devoted member of the Congregational church.

Eight weeks after signing his contract he had his plans and specifications ready for the first building, and the cornerstone laying took place as scheduled. It was a fine spring day. The elaborate ceremonies were handled by the Masonic Lodge with Augustus Baldwin in charge. Under Porter as grand Marshal in his formal uniform as militia colonel, four hundred men and women marched from David Hudson's house up the hill to the college plot. A choir sang an original hymn. Caleb Pitkin delivered a learned address in Latin, understood, it was said, by no one in the audience. The assemblage then paraded down the hill to the village church where the Reverend Stephen Bradstreet of Old Stone Church in Cleveland, and later a college trustee, spoke at length—and in English. That night the box in the cornerstone was looted and robbed. The Anti-Masons were generally blamed for the theft.

This first building on the campus was called Middle College. Before it was completed trustees were making plans for two more, one to be a double house for the president and a professor, the other, South College intended for classrooms and as a chapel. Colonel Porter was given the contract for both buildings in the spring of 1829.

That year, while Hudson was deeply involved in the pressing problems of the college, an official notice from the office of newly elected President Andrew Jackson's postmaster general informed the squire he was no longer to be the village postmaster. Hudson, a staunch Federalist, had waged outspoken opposition to Jackson's candidacy, expressing his feelings in letters to public officials and other prominent citizens. So "hoist with his own petar," he was an early victim of Old Hickory's spoils system. He sent off an indignant letter of protest to the postmaster general. But Benjamin Whedon was appointed to succeed the squire and the post office was moved from the cherry desk in the Hudson house where it had functioned for twenty-five years.

In the meantime Colonel Porter moved his family from Tallmadge to Hudson. A short time later in 1829 he died suddenly of bilious fever. After Porter's death, his son Simeon, twenty-two and well trained by his father, carried on with the President's House and Middle College.

In December 1826 three students registered. They were all male. Coeducation's day had yet to be born. But it was coming and sooner than the officials could have imagined. At the opening of Western Reserve College in the fall, twenty-two applied for the freshman class and seventeen for the preparatory department. David L. Coe, director of the academy in Tallmadge, came to Hudson to become a tutor at $300 a year. Characteristic of colleges at this time tutors handled students in the preparatory section and in the freshman and sophomore classes, while the professors taught the upper classes. Western Reserve's first professor was the Reverend Charles B. Storrs, a minister in Ravenna. His salary was $480 a year.

By 1831 three fine brick buildings, Middle College, South College, and the President's House, had risen on the hill. The college had the wholehearted support of the community and was winning recognition throughout northeastern Ohio and beyond. Well might aging Squire Hudson exclaim as his eyes overflowed with tears of gratitude: "I asked the Lord for a home in the wilderness and He gave it to me. I asked Him for a church and He gave that. But the college—the college, I never thought He would give me that—that is the child of my old age." Prospects for the college on the hill seemed bright indeed. No one could imagine that near disaster loomed ahead.

GEORGE E. PIERCE, President of Western Reserve College 1834–55.

THE FIRST COLLEGE PRESIDENTS

WESTERN RESERVE COLLEGE, launched so auspiciously in 1826, floundered six years later over an antislavery controversy: colonization versus immediate emancipation. The American Colonization Society believed a wrong could be righted by transporting freed slaves to their ancestral home on the west coast of Africa. As far back as President Jefferson's time colonization was advocated, the Virginia legislature passing several resolutions endorsing the idea. Also religious-minded colonizationists felt that since slaves were Christians they could act as missionaries bringing salvation to their fellow Africans.

David Hudson, most villagers, and the college faculty including President Storrs, all colonizationists, were caught in a violent storm with the appearance on campus of William Lloyd Garrison's stirring article in the *Liberator* pressing for immediate emancipation. College students were soon in the fray. The young professor of mathematics, the brilliant Elizur Wright, Jr., native of Tallmadge, a convert to immediate emancipation, wrote a series of articles on the subject for the *Hudson Observer and Telegraph*. Colonizationists answered, presenting their point. The editor, growing weary of the outbursts, finally closed his columns to both sides.

The controversy, however, rose to a climax when Beriah Green, professor of Sacred Literature and a fiery abolitionist, preached four so-called sermons in the chapel of the building known as South College. The colonizationists, he declared, were hypocrites since those not for emancipa-

PROFESSOR BERIAH GREEN

tion were for slavery and could not be classed as Christians. Local citizens resented Green's opprobrium and were further annoyed at his siphoning off students and faculty from the local Congregational church by requiring attendance at the college chapel. David Hudson as college trustee, joining with Caleb Pitkin, president of the board, and Harvey Coe, secretary of the board, issued a public statement lamenting the turn of events, and remained loyal members of the village church.

Criticism of Professor Green increased when he published his so-called sermons in a pamphlet that was praised by the *Liberator*. Professor Wright now contributed some articles to that publication and Western Reserve College gained national attention. The village was in an uproar. Tempers flared. Now and then fists flew as heated arguments took place on street corners, in homes, and in neighborhood gatherings. Academic life was disrupted while students as well as faculty were away lecturing on abolition. With the growing confusion on campus, parents began to remove their sons. Donors both in the Reserve and in the East where substantial sums had been promised, refused to honor pledges.

In 1833 President Storrs gave a three-hour emancipation speech in the rain at Tallmadge. Always delicate, he became very ill afterwards and a few months later died, memorialized by the Quaker poet John Greenleaf Whittier as a martyr to the cause of the Negro. (Frederick Waite, a Hudson native and later professor at the college, commented that Storrs rather was a martyr to his chronic lung affliction.) At this juncture what had started as Oberlin Collegiate Institute in Oberlin, a town to the west of Hudson, now acquired collegiate standing.

Supporters of Hudson's college saw the move a dangerous rival, for the new school was creating much attention particularly as it favored immediate emancipation. The Hudson college on its part, in attempting to quiet the slavery issue that was tearing it apart, took a neutral stand thereby satisfying neither colonizationists or abolitionists.

Oberlin shortly invited Negroes to enroll and also women. At this point, to the consternation of Hudson, Owen Brown resigned from the board of Western Reserve College and, affronting village citizens still further, sent his daughter Florilla (John's half sister) to Oberlin. He further antagonized his friends by backing what was called the Seceder, or Oberlin Church. Meetings were held in a building at the

The old Oberlin Church as it appeared in the 1950s.

southeast corner of Streetsboro and East Main streets where silver-tongued orators like the evangelist Asa Mahan expounded in lurid language on the hell that awaited those who did not make war in behalf of the shackled blacks.

Western Reserve College trustees, emerging from the slavery controversy, appointed as the new president George E. Pierce, a graduate of Yale. Differing markedly from Storrs, he was a big man, and while not fat, he tipped the scales at three hundred pounds. But he carried his weight with dignity. Too heavy for the usual horseback travel, he got about in an especially made carriage, the side where he sat sagging notably.

Pierce, ignoring the effects of a recent panic, at once began spending money. Emphasizing science he doubled the size of the

PROFESSOR ELIAS LOOMIS

faculty and appointed a professor of chemistry with an allowance of $2,500 for new equipment. He sent another, Professor Elias Loomis, to Europe with an appropriation of $4,000 to purchase a telescope and built an observatory to house it. The third in the country, the observatory did much to spread the fame of Western Reserve College. At the same time Pierce set up a medical department in Cleveland out of which a world renowned school of medicine developed.

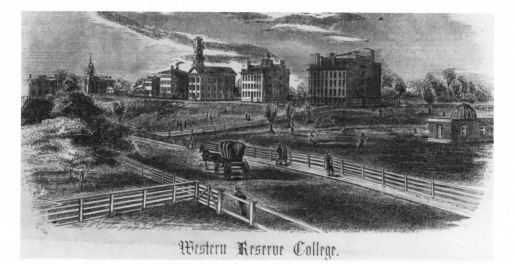

Western Reserve College.

The campus grounds were improved and fenced against wandering pigs and cows. Four new buildings were contracted for, the most outstanding the chapel. Plans for it, secured from New Haven, suggest the touch of a classic master builder such as Asher Benjamin. It was dedicated in 1836, the year David Hudson died. The tower's original top member, the victim years later of a windstorm, never has been replaced, leaving the once classic building with an awkward truncated appearance.

The first half of President Pierce's twenty-one-year presidency, with the new campus buildings and other innovations, brought acclaim and students to the college. But it was a time when money was hard to come by. Pledges were not being honored and even tuition—$30 a year—was not met promptly. The president's improvements and additions had been costly. To pay for them Pierce pursued the elusive funds often traveling in the East to collect promised accounts and not overlooking those at home base. Calling on a local farmer behind in his obligations, Pierce might point to a fat heifer in the barnyard, announcing that he would take it in lieu of what the man had pledged. So it was that the president now and then could be seen headed homeward with a farm animal hitched behind his carriage, or maybe a lamb securely trussed in the seat beside him. Thus Hudson's butcher would be supplied with fresh meat and the college with the cash he paid for it.

Enrollment that had fallen off, rose steadily with Pierce's coming in 1834. A picture of student life at the time is preserved in the diary of John Buss, a student, and later proprietor of Hudson's general store on southwest Main Street. Wood cut by the students from the college woodpile provided heat for their rooms and was kept neatly piled in their closets. In the morning they washed at the college pump, standing knee-deep in the snow in winter. Weekly board rose to $1.50 if coffee or tea, considered sinful luxuries, were included. They cooked for themselves in their rooms or ate in one of the numerous boardinghouses. They rose early, morning chapel being at seven. Infraction of the multiplicity of rules brought severe punishment, often suspension. Walking on Sunday afternoon, for example, was forbidden as well as bowling on the green, playing any games, or even riding in a sleigh for pleasure. Use of intoxicating beverages or sniffing ether, which "produced a highly exhilerating effect," were dealt with severely.

At this time the village was absorbed in a new national enthusiasm, railroads. The idea that Hudson one day would become a national railroad center was promoted by Henry N. Day, professor of Sacred Rhetoric at the college. Although Day appealed to Pierce for college backing of the concept, Pierce had too many problems of his own to get involved. He was traveling constantly in pursuit of money to meet the college debt that had reached $35,000 and was growing. His efforts had succeeded in reducing it somewhat when an eastern creditor demanded immediate payment for a $4,000 obligation that could not be ignored. The president daringly allocated the money from the sacrosanct endowment fund, which was never to be touched.

Criticism of Pierce, which had been growing, rose in a storm. He had modernized the curriculum, beautified the campus with handsome buildings that would be a permanent asset, increased the enrollment, and spread the fame of Hudson's college. But he had functioned without regard for the debt he was incurring. Calls were heard for his resignation. But he refused to step down. In 1855, however, when he reached his sixtieth birthday, the date at which he said he had planned to retire, he relinquished his post.

President Pierce's house, built in 1856 at the north end of the college campus.

In lieu of the considerable back salary due him, he accepted the Oviatt farm which had been deeded to the college for a chair of sacred literature that never had been established. It was an extensive piece of property and, like all early land, had increased in value—to the advantage of Pierce. Singularly free from the bitter criticism that had been levelled against him, Pierce bought land close to the campus, and there built his home, he and his family occupying it as long as he lived. Eventually acquired by Western Reserve Academy, ultimate successor to the college, the house designated as Pierce House, became the home of the school's headmasters.

Pierce's successor, Henry L. Hitchcock, was born in Burton, the first native Ohioan to become president of the college. Faced with a debt grown to $43,000, a staggering amount in that era, Hitchcock made collection of it his first concern, traveling constantly, often in the East to collect it. He managed to garner about $35,000, part in cash and the rest in land, which, with the pioneer era ended, had real value.

Sensitive to the growing trend toward science in the originally almost exclusively classic curriculum, he named Edward W. Morley as professor of chemistry. It was a memorable appointment. Morley put together the first laboratory west of the Alleghenies in which students actually participated. His mind evolved countless inventions and many are the Hudson tales about them. Persuading the local telegrapher to extend a line to his laboratory, he made good use of it, wiring Cleveland newspapers the college baseball score as the game ended, and, when assailed by hunger pangs, telegraphing his scholarly but absentminded wife that it was time to put the potatoes on for lunch. Acquiring one of the early Packard automobiles and as delighted as a boy with a toy, he took the car apart, knowledgeable about every nut and bolt.

Morley's fame came from his involved studies of the atmosphere and his research into its content. After the college moved to Cleveland in 1882, he teamed with Albert Michelson, professor of physics at Case School of Applied Science, the two men to become famous for their studies of ether drift in the atmosphere and the atomic weight of oxygen.

The

Miscellaneous Record,

Of David Hudson, Jr.;

Began June 13th, 1829.

In the evening, about 7 o'clock. ... After I rose this morning, I went with Milo, and helped him measure over again the distance from our Road, to the turn in the College Road.

There was a mistake in measuring the same before; it was made out to be 11 chains and odd links.

We made the distance 21 chains 42 links.

I fixed the above title while the rest were at breakfast

I spent a considerable time in looking for the mare, for father.

I was late at work both at the office both a. m, and p. m.

For a [nearly 10] considerable while, p. m, I hoed, corn principally, in the garden with Bascom and Luther.

Harvey returned last night, from his pursuit after the thief that stole Esq. Johnson's horse. He got no trace of him.

Harvey was taken sick, and is so yet.

He was bled to-day by Dr. Ladd.

Measurement of Road. Correction. Title. Search for horse.
Hoeing Corn. Harvey's Return. Sickness. Bleeding.

DAVID HUDSON JUNIOR AND
THE NEW DOCTOR

ON JANUARY 1, 1825 David Hudson junior at the age of twenty began a daily journal and continued it for more than ten years. He referred to it as "a short sketch of my life" and might have added "and of the times in which I lived." It is the chronicle of a shy, lonely young man, self-centered, frequently ill, and usually overlooked in the busy, crowded family home. Presided over by his father, David Hudson senior and his second wife, Mary, it was the home, too, of David's oldest brother, Samuel, his sister, capable Anner Maria, her husband Harvey Baldwin, and their children. Living here also, David noted in his journal, were "the hired man, Mr. Upson, several choppers who work for Harvey Baldwin, two or three boarders and two young women who are hired help."

Despite the presence of her stepmother, energetic Anner Maria took over much of the household routine. This included managing the well-stocked bar. It was a busy place, particularly as the stage passed through the town and the Hudson house was a regular stop.

From the fluent manner in which young David expresses himself in his journal, it is evident that somehow he had benefited from a good pioneer education. He was skilled enough to handle a responsible job on a newspaper, *The Western Intelligencer.* When the paper moved its offices from Hudson to Cleveland, David moved with it. He earned "$1.25 a week as a telegrapher and paid 12½ cents a night for his lodging." His boardinghouse was near Lake Erie, which was fortunate since he was forced to wash his bedstead regularly because of the bedbugs. Besides, he "enjoyed having his baths in the waves."

In Cleveland the talk everywhere was of the canal. The year David began his journal the first shovel of earth was upturned for the waterway at Newark far to the south. A great shout had gone up: the canal was on the way! David would not have known about the excitement at Newark. His father subscribed to three newspapers, the *Western Courier*, the *Religious Intelligencer*, and the *New York Spectator*. But there would have been no mention in these publications of a canal in Ohio. A Clevelander, however, Alfred Kelley, a member of the Ohio legislature, was deeply interested in the waterway, believing it would open the state to more rapid development. When David bathed in the lake he could see Kelley's home high above on a bluff overlooking the water.

David probably was not much impressed with Cleveland. Its population had been recorded in 1820 as 606. His birthplace, Hudson, was not far behind at 491. Traveling back and forth between Cleveland and Hudson David walked, a stretch of twenty-five miles or more. He walked everywhere, covering great distances. In his father's stables there were horses that could have provided transportation, but the son apparently did not have the use of one. If he was overtaken by darkness, he lighted his way with a flaming torch of dry corn husks or leaves gathered en route. Should he become weary, he stopped at a farmhouse to ask for overnight lodging. Such was pioneer hospitality that he seems never to have been turned away, although he was frequently forced to share a bed with one or two other men.

The newspaper again set up offices in Hudson, and David stayed with it, going back to live at the family home. He had grown careless about his appearance and irregular in his meals. Such habits disturbed his father who made a pact with his son: "If I would eat three meals a day and wear a wrapper and drawers every day for three months, he then would give me $5. I fulfilled the conditions and my father presented me with a handsome $5 bill."

But David was not comfortable at home. "I was spoken to at dinner," he wrote in his diary, "in a manner calculated to degrade. This excited such a disagreeable feeling I almost felt unable to do anything. I went to work, however, and made two milking stools and also cleaned out the pig pen. I told my father I calculated to make some new arrangements. He then gave me a severe lecture which wounded me and I determined to leave. But Mother told me to wait until my clothes got dried as they were being washed, and I got over the idea of going away . . . and concluded to continue printing the paper."

Relations with Harvey Baldwin, never cordial, did not improve. The domineering Baldwin made it clear he had little regard for his

Leander Starr's house on the southeast corner of the green.

brother-in-law. David, who on his part returned the feeling, wrote in his journal: "I don't like Harvey as much as some." Baldwin who was frequently ill—which may account in part for his short temper with David—often sent for the village's new doctor, Israel Town.

David, too, was ailing and becoming increasingly concerned about his health. He confided to his journal that he had bad feelings in his stomach. He suffered from colic and his head bothered him. To treat a breaking out on his skin he "made an ointment of dock root and cream." But it was not effective and before long he also would be consulting Dr. Town.

"One time," he noted, "the doctor gave me Supponatious Pills. They were in an envelope and cost 12½ cents. I left the money this afternoon." He went soon again to have the doctor "draw a blister" and later "to have a lash pulled out that I thought was in my eye. But none was seen." Yet his eyes continued to trouble him. His legs ached and he suffered from stomach pains.

The Israel Town house on East Main Street. Drawing by Ann Guldan.

Town's practice steadily increased. In 1835, after more than a decade in Hudson, he could afford to buy another parcel of land from Oviatt, half a block from the first house. Here he later built his home, a Greek Revival showcase with classic columns and a large wing on either side of the entrance. On the tax duplicate it was listed at $800.05, a large sum for a house at that time. It is attributed to the early carpenter-builder, Leander Starr who erected a similar dwelling on North Main Street for the prominent Hudson citizen, Van R. Humphrey.

The doctor, who had settled first in Cleveland, had moved to Hudson about 1823. He was influenced according to village lore by Heman Oviatt who felt the village needed this physician—and Oviatt had land to sell. Town was originally from Granville, New York. There Lucy White had won his heart and he poured out his feelings for her in letter after letter. She looked forward, she replied, "to the happy union you desire." But her parents were unwilling she should move so far away to what they believed was an untamed wilderness. "And when I reflect on the vast expanse of land and water that lies between us and consider the dangers to which we

The Van Renesselaer Humphrey house on North Main Street.

would be exposed it seems presumptious to anticipate a union."

Town, however, was not one to give up. He granted that where he lived was considerable distance from Granville. "But here it is healthful and delightful—far superior to my native village." In Hudson he expected to open a drugstore which he would operate along with his physician practice, he wrote Lucy, adding, "the citizens appear to be my friends. What business there is I will get. . . . I have boarded as yet in a commercial coffee house. My board and washing amount to 4 shillings a week." He announced that he was planning a business trip in the East. At that time he would call at Lucy's home, meet her parents, and, he hoped, bring her back with him as his wife. And all this he accomplished.

In a letter to her parents about their journey west, Lucy extolled her husband's kindness to her. At one stop he bought her some beautiful dresses, "one a black crape and also a gingham for everyday," and at Utica "a pair of high heeled Morocco slippers." They traveled "by Lake Steamer from Buffalo, reaching Ohio at Grand River. The rest of the way we came in our own wagon that the Doctor had left at his boarding place."

On their arrival in Hudson the Towns lived for some time on rented property, later buying a house from Oviatt on what became East Main Street. The price is not known but the mortgage was $241.05, in that day a sizeable sum.

The doctor kept horses and a carriage. Mrs. Town, whose health was not good, was driven about the village on pleasant afternoons, her husband feeling that these excursions in the open air benefited his delicate wife. Writing to her mother, Mrs. Town reported, "My health is better than it has been for four years. I cannot do any hard work, but my husband keeps a hired girl. I can sew and knit and visit my nearest neighbors. . . . I cannot express my gratitude for a companion who is not only able but willing to do so much for me." She wished she could visit her parents in the East "and bring my darling babies, Edward and Mary." She was not strong enough, however, to undertake the trip with the children, and unfortunately her husband could not be away from his practice for such an extended time. But Mrs. Town was homesick for her relatives in the East. Soon her younger sister, Sally, was dispatched to Hudson to cheer up the invalid.

ANSON ALVORD BREWSTER

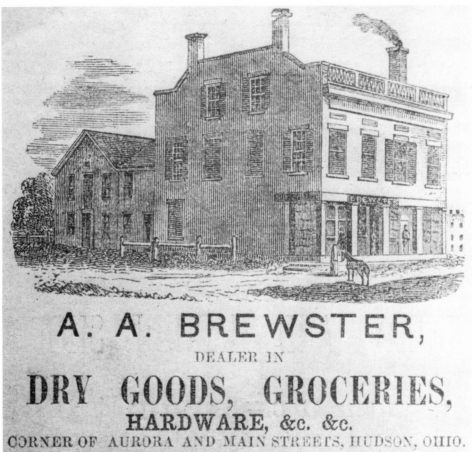

A. A. BREWSTER,

DEALER IN

DRY GOODS, GROCERIES,

HARDWARE, &c. &c.

CORNER OF AURORA AND MAIN STREETS, HUDSON, OHIO.

ANSON BREWSTER, JR., young proprietor of Kent and Brewster General Store, with the help of his clerk had placed a large wheel of cheese near the tea, coffee, and spices. Across the aisle were the yard goods, including bolts of homespun linsey-woolsey, calico, some silks and laces as well as buttons, pins, needles, and thread—everything for the dressmaker. Toward the rear of the store could be seen a modest assemblage of lamps, rugs, and furniture as well as such farm implements as shovels, wheelbarrows, rope, and rakes.

The name Kent on the signboard over the door represented the aggressive Zenas Kent of Ravenna who had supplied the capital for the store. He was a neighbor of Anson's father, Anson, Sr., and frequently had driven into Hudson, his wagon filled with farm produce that he had no trouble selling. The village, founded by the enterprising David Hudson, was forging ahead. A store here, the canny Kent decided, would be a profitable investment. Personable young Anson Brewster, Jr., had had some experience clerking for a relative in a store in Washington, D.C. In 1823 Kent picked him to handle the Hudson store, and from the outset he had been a success.

It was on a rainy afternoon, and with no customers in the store at the time, that young Brewster was standing near the front door, idly looking out. He noticed a young woman carefully making her way across the mud on Main Street, apparently headed toward his store. She was a stranger to Anson, who thought that by now he knew everyone in the village. Whoever she was, she was attractive, he noted, and he hurried to the door to welcome her. . . . Could he show her some silks, or maybe laces or cottons? he asked.

She smiled and admitted with some embarrassment that she wasn't shopping—she was only getting out of the rain that had come up suddenly. She was Sally White of Granville, New York, she volunteered and was visiting her sister Lucy, wife of Dr. Israel Town. Her sister wasn't well, and she had a little boy and girl to care for. Dr. Town engaged a hired girl, but there was a great deal to do, Sally said, adding that she helped all she could.

Brewster, introducing himself, replied that he was acquainted with the doctor and his wife, and enquired about his visitor's trip to Hudson. It had not been an easy journey, Sally declared. She had taken the stage from her home to the Erie Canal, and later, with much difficulty, boarded a Great Lakes Steamer. The lake had been very rough. She finally reached Cleveland where, after a tedious wait, she caught the stage to Hudson. She found it the most uncomfortable ride with no backs to the seats and over the worst road she ever had encountered. She would not have come, she implied, had she known how difficult the journey would be.

SARAH PORTER WHITE

But now that she was here she was enjoying herself, she admitted. She was attending one of the classes for young ladies in water color painting and embroidery. It was taught, she added, by Mrs. Rufus Nutting, wife of a professor at the college. A varied program, including the classics and other subjects was available to "young ladies" in Hudson. The village, enthusiastically supporting its college for young men was not to deny similar opportunities for the other sex, and these classes were well attended. One of the most ambitious of these ventures was at the Brick Academy on Aurora Street. It was operated by H. H. Gross who had come from Connecticut to set up the school. The youngest pupils were taught on the first floor with the older students instructed upstairs.

While Sally was taking advantage of some of these offerings, she also was giving attention to her sister Lucy. She apparently, however, had found time for diversions with other young people in the village and had written home about these good times. As a result one of her sisters, fearful she was "going to too many balls and sleigh rides," urged her "to make religion the business" of her life. Sally read the letter and saved it, for it is still in existence. But it cannot be said she heeded its advice.

Like most of the young women she had met in Hudson, Sally had a "Common Book" in which young men wrote with great effusion. In the spring of 1832 a page of six four-line verses signed "A.A.B." appeared in her book. The last stanza looked far into Sally's future:

> But when some forty years have gone
> Turn back upon this page thine eyes
> And thou will then remember one
> Whose words were prophesies.

Sally Porter White and Anson Alvord Brewster were married at Dr. Israel Town's home on October 4, 1832. The officiating clergyman was the president of Western Reserve College, the Reverend Charles B. Storrs. At the time he was caught up in the local controversy between immediate freedom of the Negro as opposed to colonization. Apparently the bitterly debated issue had no effect on the nuptials.

An inveterate letter writer, Dr. Town sent off to relatives in the East a detailed account of the wedding. After a prelude about "that monster the cholera having escaped Hudson although appearing on the Canal five miles away," Town wrote that "Lucy's health is poor." There was "a common cause," he added, "which I hope will never happen again, Viz: for some days past she has been preparing for and last night waited on about one hundred Gentlemen and Ladies who filled our house to witness the ceremony of uniting in the bonds of matrimony Mr. Anson A. Brewster and Sally White." Never overcome by modesty, he added: "The wedding party was said to be superior to anything that often occurs in this country."

"Mr. Brewster," he explained, "is a merchant . . . who owns a handsome situation about ten rods from me, a house two stories high and a store. If you send Sally any Beds or Bedding mark the boxes 'Kent and Brewster, Hudson, Ohio,' and they will come as safe as you could bring them. Since Sally has been with us she has been to a Ladies' School something more than a year and she has made good improvement. I have at all times kept a hired girl and have not made Sally other than as a sister. I think in strictness she has done well in coming to Ohio."

The Brewsters' "handsome situation about ten rods" from Dr. Town was the house Owen Brown had built and occupied near the corner of Aurora and Main streets, part of the extensive property he owned. It was apparently a commodious building, adequate to house the Brewsters and their numerous children, who arrived in quick succession. Owen Brown had lost a wife and child when he lived there and tragedy was to strike the Brewsters.

The Baldwin-Buss house was built in 1825 by Augustus Baldwin.

An integral part of the Brewster chronicle is the saga of the young Englishman, John Buss. He had come to Hudson to attend Western

Reserve College and there to prepare for the ministry. His eyes were not equal to the strain of the studying required, he noted in his diary—or did the curriculum make heavier academic demands than he could manage? At any rate, he gave up his scholastic plans, took out naturalization papers, and became a permanent citizen of Hudson.

A friendly, gossipy individual, he seems to have known everyone in the village—and all about them. Brewster, for example, according to Buss, had lost the sight of one eye in a shooting accident. But Buss declared he could see more with that one eye than most people saw with two! Buss left a valuable legacy, a diary in which he recorded the town's daily events; he maintained the record from 1833 until his death. Buss had no difficulty finding employment. After trying out several other jobs he began working as a clerk for Brewster in 1836. The pay was eighteen dollars a month, soon raised to twenty. This included board and washing as well as a certain amount of clothing at cost from the store. It was the start of a long association with Brewster, frequently broken off, but always resumed.

Brewster found that business was good. Before long he bought out Kent's interest and was able to establish his own store at the corner of Aurora and Main streets. Within a few years he would house it in a fine brick building with living quarters on the second floor. (John Buss, having developed a personal satisfaction in the expanding program, proudly noted in his diary: "Bricks for the store are now being laid.") On the Main Street side there would appear: "BREWSTER'S" in big bold letters.

One cold January night Hudson's quiet darkness was pierced with the cry of "Fire! Fire!" The Owen Brown house was in flames. The fire, as so often was the case in pioneer days, originated in the house's chimney. First to respond to the outcry was Buss. Marshalling the men who had come to help, Buss had Sally and her baby carried out of the burning house on a mattress. Depositing them, mattress and all, at the nearby home of Frederick Baldwin, Buss later moved them a few doors away to Dr. Town's house where Sally's sister took charge. And in his journal John Buss commented gratefully that the flames had not reached the Brewster Store.

Brewster, now very much in need of a home for his family, purchased property at the corner of College and Division streets. The land originally was part of a large tract that had been deeded to Western Reserve College by Heman Oviatt. Losing no time,

Brewster had a commodious brick house erected during the summer of 1843. This was to be the Brewsters' home while the store and quarters above it were being built. The house and lot, originally valued at $450, were eventually sold by Brewster to Charles W. Farrar for $1,000. Farrar made stoves, small room-sized affairs, that found a ready market. Later Farrar worked for Brewster in the store.

Sally, meanwhile, was giving birth to a succession of babies. In a letter to one of her sisters in the East she explains she had "not written sooner because I have not been well since the birth of my last baby. . . . She is eight weeks old now. . . . I cannot sit up all day and am not able to do anything except sew a little." Sally's babies were welcomed and loved. She had eight all told; the first several were girls, and Anson wanted a son who could carry on the business that he had inaugurated so successfully. When the long awaited son arrived, they named him John Buckingham Brewster. Described as "a very lively little boy," he seemingly sensed the paternal favoritism. As soon as he could walk he followed his father everywhere, getting into trouble in the store amidst the crates and barrels, begging to go along when his father drove off on a local errand.

Photograph of village green taken in 1861 by John Markillie.

With his business well launched, Brewster could give attention to village issues. Joining with other prominent citizens, including Henry O'Brien and Dr. Town, he helped organize the local Episcopal church, a denomination of which he had long been a member. Meetings at first were held in the Brewster home above the store and later, as membership increased, in the Brick Academy. The Reverend T. B. Fairchild of Cuyahoga Falls alternated for the Sunday service with the Reverend G. S. Davis of Franklin Mills. Membership that had started with a few communicants steadily increased, and, largely through the efforts of the women of the church, an organ was purchased.

Suddenly the well-ordered life of the Brewsters was jolted by tragedy. In December 1841 a virulent form of scarlet fever, rampant throughout the area, attacked four-year-old John, who became very ill. His father, then on a buying trip in New York, was sent for. John Buss, seemingly always available in an emergency, noted in his diary that he spent all Christmas day "with Brewster at little John's bedside."

Two days after Christmas Anson Brewster's father, also named Anson, who lived on a farm near Ravenna, wrote in his Daybook: "I was called upon this morning to go to Hudson to attend the funeral of my little grandson, John Buckingham Brewster who died of scarlet fever. . . . I am distressed beyond measure." Four days later he had additional tragic news to record: his one-year-old granddaughter Lucy, little John's sister, had contracted the fever and died, "and is to be buried this morning. Her sister, Martha, is dangerously ill with the same disease. . . . Their mother, Sally," he added, "was put to bed with a living daughter." As he waited for further word from Hudson he "was almost distracted" and stayed with Joseph Hines at night. On New Year's day (1842) he noted in his diary: "Myself and Socrates [his hired man] were alone all day expecting to hear more from Hudson." He "spent the night again with Hines. Not one of our other neighbors have been here to enquire about our troubles." On January 3 he noted in his Daybook: "My wife returned, driven home by Luther Curtis. She brought word that Martha was alive and Sally and her child doing well."

Drawing by Horace Rogers of the Brewster Mansion
designed by Simeon Porter and constructed by F. W. Bunnell.

In 1850 Simeon Porter, recently established in the Cleveland
architectural firm of Porter and Heard, was brought in to design a
new house suitable to the Brewster family's ever increasing
prominence in town. The imposing new building, with its elegant
stone front and Gothic turrets in the very latest style, was surely
admired by the townspeople, and Sally Brewster was glad to leave
the scene of the tragic deaths of her two babies and start afresh in
her lovely new home.

Meanwhile, Brewster was caught up in "railroad fever," and shared
with many villagers the conviction that Hudson someday would be

Four of Sally and Anson Brewster's daughters in later years.
From left, seated: Hattie, Alice, Lucy, and *standing,* Mary Helen.

a thriving metropolis. With such a future in mind he bought up considerable village property, including much of what had been Owen Brown's holdings, as well as some Main Street locations. By 1857 the railroad bubble had burst. However, Brewster was a rich man. He died suddenly from a heart attack in 1864, when the Civil War was taking the lives of so many Americans and the Republican National Convention had nominated Abraham Lincoln for reelection. Brewster's widow and his unmarried daughters continued to live in what always was referred to as the Brewster Mansion.

ANNER MARIA HUDSON BALDWIN

HARVEY BALDWIN

HUDSON DIES, COLLEGE EXPANDS, VILLAGE INCORPORATES

WITH THE ABLE Porter brothers at hand, Western Reserve College president George E. Pierce started at once on plans for a chapel as the first of the new college buildings. It was to be multi-purpose, providing for a college church, theological department, and library. Simeon Porter was twenty-seven when he signed the contract, with Orrin Porter as assistant. Recent research by Eric Johannesen reveals that Porter's design followed that of Yale's first chapel. Built in 1762 and since demolished, it had a chapel and gallery on the first two floors, with the third given to the library. Porter, according to Johannesen, using the upper floors for the chapel and the first floor for the library, turned the Yale building upside down! But that structure was "a typical colonial meeting house," while Porter's is Greek, "evidence of the Greek Revival style fanning out to the frontier from a center like New Haven." From the time of this "copy" Western Reserve College came to be called "the Yale of the West." And, of course, the president, several trustees, and faculty members were also New Haven men.

David Hudson was seventy-five and failing. He took great satisfaction in the chapel going up on his campus. One wonders, since he was so well informed about the affairs of the area, if he was also following the progress of another significant religious edifice, the Mormon Temple, being built in Kirtland, twenty miles away. Both buildings testify today to the high achievement of the early craftsmen.

On Thursday afternoon, March 17, Hudsonites picking up their *Ohio Observers* were shocked and saddened to read the following:

DEATH OF DEACON DAVID HUDSON

This venerable *patriarch* died at 3 o'clock this afternoon, aged 75 years. In this death the church in Hudson has been bereft of a consistent member—the W R College of a valuable patron and Trustee—and the cause of humanity and benevolence, of a warm and liberal supporter. "Mark the perfect man and behold the upright: for the end of that man is peace." The funeral will be attended at the Congregational Meeting House, day after to morrow (19th) at 11 o'clock A.M. The procession will be formed at the dwelling house at 10 o'clock and will move to the church, where a discourse will be delivered. The relatives and friends of the deceased—the Trustees, officers and friends of the W R College are requested to attend.

Evidently all who were requested to attend did, and many more. As the young John Buss, then a student at the college noted in his diary, "I think there were more people at his funeral than I ever saw before at once except once in England." Meanwhile the eloquent young David Hudson junior recorded the scene at home as follows:

My father—Dead!!—He has been more than usually unwell for a few days past. His ailment was extreme weakness; he was easily exhausted. He took his bed last night, and kept it till his death. This morning he called the family together, and spoke his last words to them, giving directions respecting his burial and stating that he did not expect to continue but a little while. This afternoon, the family were suddenly called into the room; he was in a distressed turn, occasioned by coughing. He could not withstand it, but sunk under it. Exertions were made, with the utmost anxiety, to bring him to; but all in vain: he struggled, and sunk into death, to the anguish of mother, and the tears and sobs of the family. He died about 2 o'clock. He was 75 years the 17th of last February.

The day of the funeral the whole family gathered. Young David wrote that "all my brothers and sisters attended [the service], except Samuel, whom I tried to make go, but could not." Prayers were

said at the house before the procession filed solemnly to the meetinghouse to listen to "numerous discourses" and more prayers. John Buss finished his entry for the day: "Mr. Doolittle preached the sermon text, the memory of the just is blessed, it was a good sermon. May the Lord grant that the mantle of Esq. Hudson may fall upon his successors in every department of life." David Hudson was gone, but he had left his town and college flourishing. As the *Observer* noted in a later eulogy, "He has erected a monument, which it is believed, will long endure and for which future generations will rise up and call him blessed." This comment refers only to the college, but surely applies to the town as well.

Wills, particularly of the prominent, always arouse interest, David Hudson's more than most. While the squire was recognized as a man of wealth, its extent was probably surprising to his fellow townspeople. Hudson's widow was to have one-third of the estate as her dower, which, it appeared, after her death was to go to Anner Maria and her husband Harvey Baldwin. The squire treated them as one, evidence of the high regard in which he held his daughter and son-in-law. The Baldwins' legacies were the largest—a very substantial amount consisting of "all the lands owned by me in the Township of Hudson, including all improvements and buildings thereon." Further, the will obligated Anner and her husband to care for certain family members like Samuel who was to be "suitably supported during his lifetime by them." They were also to oversee the youngest son, David, and the land provided for him, but he survived his father by less than two months. The Ohio *Observer* reported on May 19, 1836 the following: "Died: In Chester, on Saturday, May 14, Mr. David Hudson, son of the late Dea. Hudson of this town in the 31st year of his age. Mr. Hudson has heretofore been employed, for a considerable time, in our printing office, and has always sustained the character of a meek and humble Christian. His death was sudden, although he had been declining in health for a long time. He had requested the family to retire from the room that he might get a little sleep; when they returned they found that he had fallen asleep, never more to awake in this world."

Under the terms of the will, David Hudson's considerable land holdings in Medina and Geauga counties were to be divided equally among sons William, Milo, and Timothy. And their sister Abigail Oviatt was granted a modest bequest of promissory notes and cash. The last item in the will is intriguing: "If in case my grandson, Frederick A. Hudson shall return to the path of rectitude, from which he has widely strayed; and become, in the opinion of my sons, William M. Hudson, Milo L. Hudson, Timothy Hudson, and of my daughters Abigail L. Oviatt and Anna M. Baldwin an honest useful and worthy member of society, I do recommend that they do each of them severally pay over to him the said Frederick A. Hudson Fifty Dollars cash."

According to family tradition, Anner and her husband when first married lived for a time on a Baldwin farm off West Prospect Street. But before long they seem to have taken up residence at the Hudson house where they lived out their long lives. With his inheritance, Baldwin moved into David Hudson's role as first citizen of the town, taking on former responsibilities of his father-in-law in civic and church matters as well as becoming trustee of the college, a position in which he served for forty years.

Through the years, the Baldwins' duties multiplied, and the household in the Hudson house increased. Anner's sister, Abigail Laura, divorced from Birdsey Norton Oviatt when a young woman,

Anner Maria surrounded by family on her ninetieth birthday.

had lived at the Hudson house since 1821. The Baldwin's granddaughter Anna Gregory Lee from Toledo joined the family after the death of her husband, lovingly bringing her five children. Anner, who seems to have acquired much of her father's management ability, presided over the big clan, a capable matriarch, respected and admired by everyone. At her ninetieth birthday in 1890, the citizenry turned out four hundred strong to honor this woman who had seen her birthplace develop from a small settlement in an untracked wilderness into a town enjoying all the sophisticated advancement and conveniences of the late nineteenth century.

The village's incorporation in 1837 stirred up much discussion, and ushered in many changes. The first election by "male freeholders" took place in the meetinghouse. Heman Oviatt, receiving the most votes, nineteen, became Hudson's first mayor, and Lyman Hall, with eighteen votes, the recorder. Those receiving the five next highest votes were trustees, or councilmen. The 1837 tax duplicate, first in the town records, listed seventy-two taxpayers. Highest property valuation ($10,540) was that of John B. Clark, for houses, lands, and personal property. He owned a great deal of land, part of the

The John B. Clarke house is seen in the distance in this old Main Street view.

original extensive Gaylord holdings in the area that became John Clark Lane. His handsome house was said to have been built in 1835 by Simeon Porter on grounds that became a mere remnant of the original Clark estate. Harvey Baldwin's property valuation was the second highest at $8,800. The nationwide depression was apparent in a drop from a total tax assessment of $113,441.58 in 1837 to $42,604.00 seven years later.

Sidewalks occupied much of the time of early councils. The first walks laid along the west side of Main Street were four feet wide, constructed of hewed lumber over apparently a brick underpinning. Property owners maintained the walks passing their homes or business places, Owen Brown and Harvey Baldwin, for example, each paying $20 sidewalk tax. The walks were not too sturdy, it would appear. Frequent complaints were brought before council of loose boards that, when stepped on, had a way of flying up in the faces of pedestrians. And the boards were seen to tremble when big President Pierce strode over them. The sidewalks were soon extended throughout the village and became more elaborate, built of "good oak flooring with posts and railings to help those abroad

after dark." They also served as a protection against stray livestock. Wandering animals were a continual nuisance judging from the many ordinances on the books. In vain did council pass resolutions that "every one must keep his swine out of public streets." For a dollar a year rent, Owen Brown provided a pound at the corner of what became Clinton and Main streets. Here authorities incarcerated "any horse, gelding, mare, mule, meat cattle (milch cows excepted), sheep, swine and geese found at large." Owners could reclaim their animals by paying the pound keeper 25 cents. Fines from two dollars to four dollars were issued to anyone "hitching a horse to a tree or someone's fence, or driving a horse or team in such a manner as to trample upon sidewalks or the Green."

In the latter part of November 1837, the slow-moving news reached Hudson of the murder ten days before in Alton, Illinois, of Elijah Lovejoy. The abolitionist editor died at the hands of a proslavery mob. The nation was roused. Mass meetings took place in big cities and small towns. The antislavery cause gained recruits by the hundreds. In Hudson, Laurens P. Hickock, professor of theology at Western Reserve College, previously little concerned with the Negro question, saddled his horse, and rode through the township summoning residents to a meeting in Lovejoy's name at the Congregational church.

The next afternoon the largest gathering ever seated in the meetinghouse crowded into the pews. The usually restrained Hickock opened the program with an emotional declaration, "The crisis has come!" One moving speech after another followed. Owen Brown, though shackled by stammering, extolled the editor's courage in being shot down, musket in hand, while defending his printing press. Owen closed with a long prayer, moved to flowing tears by his own eloquence. Lora Case, who was present, records that John Brown, in Hudson on a visit, sat at the rear of the auditorium. He rose when his father finished, and, raising his right hand, said "in his calm, emphatic way: 'I pledge myself with God's help that I will devote my life to increasing hostility against slavery.' " He had taken the first step in his long journey to Harpers Ferry.

In the meantime, President Pierce was pursuing his objective of college enhancement. Elias Loomis, who had been enticed from Yale to become professor of mathematics and natural philosophy at the

An early view of the Loomis Observatory.

Hudson campus, was sent to Europe to study his subject and purchase apparatus for an observatory. The small, domed building, second oldest observatory still standing in the United States, was completed by the Porters in 1838. Fine, English-made instruments, including a telescope, brought back by Loomis were installed. His pioneering work carried on here brought the college national recognition in the scientific field.

President Pierce's ambitious program was costly. The next building, the largest to date, and intended for the natural sciences, was the Athenaeum. It was slated to go up on the north campus, but its construction was delayed for three years because of lack of funds. Financial problems that would engulf Pierce's last decade as college president were casting their shadows.

HENRY NOBLE DAY

A NEW ELLSWORTH BABY AND
HUDSON'S RAILROAD ERA

DEFTLY GUIDING HIS wheelchair over the ramp connecting his house and store on East Main Street, Edgar Birge Ellsworth (known generally as Birge) announced proudly to his customers: "Mary had another baby last night—she wants to name him James William." The baby had a brother Edward, who was two. There would be two more brothers, Henry and Frank, regularly spaced at two-year intervals. When he was young, Birge had had an infection in his leg that was treated with over-applications of blue mass or mercury, a popular remedy of the day. The leg did not heal, and the usual procedure in such situations, amputation, was resorted to. Like his father, Elisha Ellsworth, Birge became a cripple, using a cane at first, eventually resorting to a wheelchair which he found more comfortable.

Photograph of Main Street looking south by John Markillie.

On this October day in 1849 with the village trees decked out in autumn's flamboyance as if to welcome the new baby, Hudson was heading into a period of booming prosperity—a circumstance prophetic of little James's destiny. The baby's father, in no way slowed up by his handicap, at thirty-five was a man of means by pioneer standards. His house and store were valued at $2,130 on tax records. In addition, he owned 200 acres in separate parcels in various sections of the township.

Some years before, confident of Hudson's future, he had bought his house and store from his father-in-law, William Dawes, descended from the William Dawes who had spread the alarm with Paul Revere. The classic house was the work of Lemuel Porter. After Porter's death, Leander Starr, who had worked for Porter, went into business for himself, putting up outstanding buildings including the Brewster

Store and residence of Edgar Birge Ellsworth.

store built two years before Ellsworth's. Originally Birge's house was the home of Norman Baldwin who had moved to Cleveland where he became a prominent businessman. Birge's store was a smaller rendering of the one built for A. A. Brewster at the corner of Aurora Street and the Cleveland Road.

Birge was a commission merchant. The large farms surrounding Hudson produced grain, dairy products, and "meat on the hoof"— enough for local consumption and for wider markets as well. Birge supplied the farmers' needs, bought their surplus including hogs and other animals which he arranged to have driven overland for higher prices in eastern markets.

Little James Ellsworth was born just as Hudson, midway into the nineteenth century and about to celebrate its semi-centennial, was caught up in the new national obsession: railroads. The unlikely local promoter, Henry N. Day, a Yale graduate, was professor of sacred rhetoric at Western Reserve College, the chair endowed by Heman Oviatt. Influenced by the profitable enterprises of his brothers in Florida, Day was ready to exchange his $700 a year college salary for the more promising prospect of a business career. He took a position as assistant at the *Ohio Observer*, published in Hudson, and within a year was in charge of the whole operation as senior partner. But railroads, the new form of transportation being talked about everywhere, were to offer the enterprising Day a more rewarding challenge.

VAN RENESSELAER HUMPHREY

Neighboring Cleveland was backing roads that would rush passengers and freight to Columbus, and indeed all the way to the Ohio River at thirty miles an hour. It appeared the lumbering stagecoach would one day be relegated to back roads. Tavern keepers and canal operators were beginning to worry about their future.

In 1836 a charter endorsed by Heman Oviatt and Judge Van R. Humphrey had been issued for the Cleveland and Pittsburgh Railroad that would pass through Hudson. But a general panic stopped its development. With the current interest in railroads, Day promoted revival of the road. He had a winning personality, his position at the college had given him a certain status, and citizens had confidence in him. Soon he managed to be appointed special agent for the contemplated line and was sent east to raise money for it—$200,000 was the suggested necessary amount. His expenses of a dollar a day were to come from this sum.

Returning to Hudson having garnered nothing like the hoped-for money, Day nonetheless held forth eloquently about the railroad, declaring it would transport Hudson's agricultural output, handle Ohio coal, and altogether make Hudson a metropolitan commercial center. The former professor soon was made a director of the proposed road.

County commissioners were persuaded to endorse a subscription plan for capital stock—with voters' approval. Bonds were issued. Local citizens hurried to buy the stock and village taxes were raised to underwrite the interest.

But before the railroad plan, the energetic Day had gotten another scheme under way. Believing what he preached—that Hudson before long would become a great commercial center—he had planned to build a business block on the northwest corner of College and Aurora streets. As his concept enlarged he applied to the college for a $3,000 loan, and was turned down. But he went ahead anyway, putting up a massive three-story structure. It was built by Frederick W. Bunnell, busy architect-builder in Hudson before the Civil War. The building was five-sided as dictated by the shape of the lot— hence its name, the Pentagon. Day finished it at a cost of $18,000. No one knew where the money had come from. It was an impressive example of Day's ability to manipulate credit. Construction began the year James Ellsworth was born; sixty years later he would order it torn down.

The Pentagon filled rapidly with tenants in all of whose businesses Day was financially involved, including Sawyer, Ingersoll, publishing and printing; a dry goods store; the *Ohio Observer;* the newspaper and printing office for the college; a drugstore; furniture and agricultural supplies; and a watchmaker and jewelry store.

Train on viaduct over Tinker's Creek in Bedford circa 1865.
Courtesy of the Western Reserve Historical Society.

By 1851 the shiny rails of the Cleveland and Pittsburgh Railroad were coming nearer Hudson, bringing promise of the new era Day had foretold, and reassurance to allay any doubts about Day himself. Finally the road was completed and the first train headed into Hudson. With its brass-trimmed locomotive belching clouds of smoke and its new bell clanging raucously, the train puffed into the depot at Railroad Street and shuddered to a stop. It seemed that all the citizens of the township had turned out to gaze at the marvel. Farmers drove in from the country to see it and had the greatest difficulty controlling their horses, terrified at the noisy monster. Mayor Van Humphrey delivered an eloquent address of welcome.

Old depot on Railroad Street circa 1870.

True to Day's prediction there was an almost immediate upsurge of activity in the village. Near the depot a planing mill and lumber yard were going up. As a sideline the company was to handle coal coming by rail from Pennsylvania. A flour mill as well as a butter and cheese warehouse soon were built.

New people began coming to Hudson, stimulating a building boom for houses. With land needed for the new houses, Day, gaining the backing of some of the village's most prominent men, bought—on credit—a large piece of land outside the village limits. It was referred to as Day's Addition.

The building and sale of the houses had to be underwritten. For this the ingenious Day created a bank, which he named The Society for Savings. He of course named himself president. Harvey Baldwin was made director. Because Baldwin had virtually taken his father-in-law's place as the village leader after David Hudson's death, his identity with the bank was a smart move on Day's part. Moses Messer, well-known dealer in lumber and building supplies, was appointed secretary-treasurer.

The "Bank" had no money but was to depend on capital from the rise in land values expected to come in Day's Addition. Day in partnership with J. W. Smith organized the mill and warehouse complex near the depot on Railroad Street.

With the first railroad having stimulated the economy so markedly, Day reasoned that a second road would be of additional

EDGAR BIRGE ELLSWORTH

advantage and in 1852 the Clinton line was launched. It was to run east from Hudson to Kinsman and on to Pennsylvania, there to connect with the Venango line. The next year the Clinton Air line was planned to head west to Tiffin where it would join a road not yet built, but which was to reach to Iowa. Before long Day and Judge Humphrey as his associate were advocating a third line, this the Hudson-Painesville line, thus giving the village an outlet on Lake Erie. By 1854 Hudson—on paper at least—was assured a future as a pivot in a transcontinental railroad network. That year Birge Ellsworth was elected village mayor. It was not known whether or not he was caught up in this railroad euphoria, but most of the citizens were. They donated land for the rights-of-way of the Clinton lines, dipped deeply into their savings, mortgaged their homes and farms, and emptied their pockets to buy stock in the lines.

Work on the first Clinton road began at once. Soon the outline of the route could be seen cutting through fields and forests. Grading and the expert stone work on bridges and culverts soon were well under way. Before long, however, it became apparent that costs were exceeding estimates. Additional funds were called for, but villagers' coffers were empty. Even Day's relatives, who heretofore had backed him readily when he was in a tight situation, were having money problems. All work on the road was abandoned by 1855.

The village soon reeled under more bad news, this time from the Pentagon. One by one the firms in the building closed in bankruptcy. Day was involved in all of them. The Hudson Society for Savings, the bank which never had been a bank, soon failed. Day's Addition lay fallow. There had been no property sales there. Day had piled credit on credit and the structure finally collapsed. Local estimates of his total indebtedness vary, but it was a staggering sum. His obligation to his brothers and to other relatives alone was said to be close to $200,000.

After wrestling for three years with a tangle of lawsuits and a pile of claims against him, Day left Hudson for Cincinnati to become president of the Ohio Female College. But it closed its doors in a few years and he returned to his home town, New Haven, to write text books on bookkeeping and ethics.

The college revived under President Pierce's successor, Henry L.

Hitchcock who freed it from debt and increased enrollment. The academy, a college-preparatory adjunct of the institution, was put on a sound basis and the teen-aged James Ellsworth was enrolled in it. A family friend, impressed with young James, suggested to his mother that he should go on to the college to prepare for the ministry. The idea horrified the boy, he confessed later because it was business that interested him. He spent a great deal of time in his father's store, becoming a real help to his crippled parent. He took part-time jobs, too, in the local stores.

Hudson's original railroad, known as the Pennsylvania Line, surviving the village's difficulties, was a valuable local asset. Birge sent his cattle to eastern markets by rail, his son James often going along to help. Shortly James was entrusted with sole management of a consignment of hogs. The boy had noticed that the animals always had been weighed first, and then watered. This time at the Buffalo stockyards he arranged to have his hogs weighed after they were watered, their increased poundage adding to the price they brought. Listening to this report on the boy's return, his father conceded that his son was not a potential clergyman.

The railroad that Birge Ellsworth found so useful was to travel some years later over tracks on high, impregnable embankments that disfigured three areas of the village. In 1902 the Pennsylvania Railroad, to eliminate its street-level tracks including the spur to the Railroad Street depot, notified the village of the changes and presented the prospectus to the council. This communication is missing from village files, but the *Hudson Independent* for November 28, 1902 printed the details.

The plan called for all railroad tracks to be carried on high bridges spanning highways. The bridge over South Main Street would be of substantial construction, giving a vertical clearance over the roadway of fourteen feet. It would be supported by solid masonry abutments parallel with the street and fifty feet apart, the width of the resulting highway. There would be no post or pillar in the center supporting the bridge as railway officials first suggested. The Pennsylvania Railroad would construct a sidewalk four feet wide the full length of the west abutment. It would be of sawed flagging equal to Peninsula stone. A walkway, it was suggested, should be provided by the village the length of the east abutment.

Over Streetsboro Street, referred to as "the Peninsula Road," a similar bridge was to be built but a more massive one to accommodate both the Cleveland and Pittsburgh line as well as the more recent Cleveland, Akron, and Columbus line. Vertical clearance above the highway was fourteen feet here. Sidewalks of the same Peninsula stone were to be provided beside the abutments on both sides of the highway.

Brown Street did not fare as well. The overpass had a clearance of only twelve feet with twenty feet for the highway between the abutments. Sidewalks were to be built by the railroad to connect with what were already there or what someday might be provided by the village.

According to the newspaper, the Hudson council and Mayor E. L. Fillius had misgivings about the railroad's proposition and held seven sessions discussing the subject. The railroad hierarchy, according to the newspaper, was impatient at the village council delay and issued an ultimatum: Hudson was either to accept the company's proposition or face a lawsuit. Village leaders, evidently concluding they could win no such litigation against so powerful an adversary, capitulated and passed the desired ordinance. In an editorial comment at the end of the article the *Independent* noted: "no one can deny that Council took plenty of time for the deliberations and did the best they could." Thus the unsightly high-borne spans and highway traffic problems remain as permanent legacies of Hudson's railroad era.

THE RETURN

ON A WINTRY day toward the end of 1888 a tall, austere man with a delicate small boy by the hand alighted from the train at Hudson's Railroad Street depot. Skipping around them a merry little girl scarcely out of babyhood mischievously evaded efforts of a young woman, evidently her governess, to corral her. With a no-nonsense air, the man marshalled the group into a waiting carriage, the best that Hudson's livery stable could produce. With their considerable luggage piled into a second rig, the cavalcade headed east to a farm on Aurora Road.

James W. Ellsworth, coal baron, bank and railroad director with numerous other business connections, had come from Chicago, his adopted city, to bring his two children "home": eight-year-old Linn (later he was to call himself Lincoln, thus annoying his uncle William Linn for whom he was named) and his sister Clare, who was three. A few weeks before pneumonia had taken the young wife and mother, the former Eva Butler, daughter of a Chicago paper manufacturer. The distraught father was giving his children the best comfort he could devise, a mother substitute—his own mother.

A widow, she was living in what the family liked to term "the Ellsworth homestead," an angular not to say ugly red brick house set amidst considerable acreage. Her late husband, the thrifty Edgar Birge Ellsworth, through the years had added to the land developing it into a valuable working farm. Their illustrious son, involved in his far-flung enterprises, returned to Hudson only rarely. The town he encountered in 1888 was changing. The once prosperous and culturally enriched trading center, quickened for more than half a century by Western Reserve College in its midst, had lost the college and had become a sleepy village, commercially stagnant, its population shrunken.

The college that in a real sense had "made" Hudson had moved to Cleveland to become Western Reserve University. The original campus and fine old buildings remained, as Western Reserve Academy. It was in part subsidized by the university, which expected academy graduates to move on into the Cleveland institution. But few of the boys were going on with their education, and, like similar

academies elsewhere, its enrollment was being cut into by the emerging public high schools. The Hudson academy like the village was on a downhill course.

Leaving his family with his mother, Ellsworth went back to Chicago but returned to Hudson in the spring, and in his usual decisive manner bundled them all—children, mother, governess—off to Europe. In those days a trip abroad was a rarity for most Americans but not for James W. Ellsworth with his expanding international contacts. They sailed on the North German Lloyd luxury line and made a fast crossing, twelve days. At times the ship had hoisted a mainsail to help the propeller.

Settling his charges in a London hotel at Trafalgar Square, Ellsworth was off to the Continent on business, with a stop in Paris

to acquire Rembrandt's *Portrait of a Man*—he had not slept for three nights "because of my desire for its possession," he is quoted as saying. Accustomed to getting what he wanted, he overcame the reluctance of the owner, a titled French woman, to part with it. Meeting the very substantial price she asked, he took the painting off her wall and trundled it back to the hotel. On the return to America he kept the picture in his stateroom.

Things of beauty were essential to him. In his reminiscences he described one of his Chinese porcelains "with its appeal in texture and color like some precious gift of nature to become a joy forever." According to his son he was an indefatigable collector but a discriminating one.

A view of rebuilt Main Street after fire of 1892.

He settled his son and daughter in Hudson with their governess in charge after his mother's death in 1891. Linn, in his autobiography *Beyond Horizons* (1938), described the house with a porch across the front, a gloomy parlor, icy cold in winter with lugubrious, prickly hair cloth furniture, "everlasting" flowers under a glass dome, and tall, dried cattails in a bouquet before the empty fireplace. The sitting room, on the other hand, had a cheery coal baseburner, comfortable, much-used chairs that creaked with each rocking, and a gay, much-worn carpet of bright cabbage roses.

The farm's offerings were a delight to the two city children: horses, stock as well as work animals, cows and sheep, barns to play in, a clear stream emptying into a small pond. For playmates Linn and Clare had their cousins Ruby and Henry, children of their father's brother Henry and his wife the former Emma Chamberlain, who lived a few miles away on Stow Road. Young Henry played the violin. In fact violins later became almost an obsession with him. It was doubtless that because of this influence Linn's father imported a violin teacher from Cleveland for his son. Unlike his cousin, Linn hated the lessons, the teacher, and the required practicing— everything in fact connected with the instrument. At the termination of the lessons he "hung up the fiddle and bow forever—with the greatest of relief," he admitted.

With his children settled in Hudson, Ellsworth was spending more time there, stopping off between trips around the country and abroad. Characteristically he instituted improvements in the home place. He remodeled the house, softening its awkward angles with wings in Queen Anne semblance and generally beautifying its exterior and interior. The farmstead, which he called Evamere in memory of his wife, was to be his summer home for years. He created a sizeable lake that he called Evamere Lake, stocking it with Muscovy ducks. Swans and peacocks roamed about the grounds, and at breeding time chased the children menacingly. In Chicago Linn and Clare had played with a goat at the home of their cousins, and their father provided a goat for them at Evamere. They also had a pony and cart as well as bantam chickens. Linn, however, heartily disliked his grandmother's little black-and-tan "rat terrier" dog that nipped at his heels, and, he confessed, it turned him forever against dogs.

The brother and sister were constant companions. In contrast to the lively Clare, her brother, who one day would defy the Arctic, was shy and physically anything but robust. Nonetheless he dreamed of becoming an athlete. The driveway at Evamere, a hard cinder road, was just 100 yards long, he discovered. At once he utilized it as a running track and soon was growing stronger from the exercise in the country environment. Bicycles were the vogue and Linn was given one. Before long he was able to peddle to Cleveland and back, twenty-five miles each way, a very real achievement over the wretched roads of the day.

Their father's remodeling of the house netted Clare and her brother each a splendidly furnished bedroom. Linn's in what had been the attic, contained a large globe map of the earth. From the big high windows in his room the stars and the moon in the clear country air were easily seen. In a play-school game he lectured his sister on going up in a balloon to the moon, visiting maybe a star or two and from there looking down on the earth and the countries shown on his globe. This boyish daydreaming must be considered prophetic, for in 1926 he was indeed to look down on the world, the unexplored Arctic from the dirigible *Norge*.

Old Public School. Hudson, Ohio.

The Hudson Union School on Oviatt Street.

In the meantime there was school, a district school in Hudson village. Linn was almost ten but to his humiliation was put in the first grade. After an unhappy period, which he called "the McGuffey years," he persuaded his father to send him to the academy. He was an indifferent student at the academy, as he was later at Yale. His special Hudson school friend was John Findlay, later minister of the Hudson Congregational Church. The two boys spent hours together on the fine tennis court Ellsworth had built at Evamere.

On each visit to Hudson Ellsworth carried out more improvements at the farm, not alone to make a pleasant home for his children, but more and more, it was clear, because the old place appealed to him. Further, it gave scope to his creative urge and his passion for perfection. Finding the road from the village to the farm rutted and in bad repair, making travel difficult for his carriages and fine

horses, Ellsworth obtained village permission to widen and repair the thoroughfare and to line both sides with fine specimens of elm trees. Trees were a major interest all his life, one of the several characteristics he shared with John D. Rockefeller whom he knew through their wide-ranging financial activities. The oil magnate at this time was setting out trees at his summer home, Forest Hills, in Cleveland.

In 1892 Ellsworth took his two children to Chicago to see the new home on Michigan Avenue, built, his son thought, primarily to house Ellsworth's art collection that had outgrown the former house. Paintings, Chinese porcelains, and other rarities overflowed the gallery into practically every room in the big house. Linn, now beginning to call himself Lincoln, found in the library a treasure trove—huge atlases. Lying for hours on his stomach on the floor he pored over the outsize maps of the world, fascinated with patches at the Poles, designated as "Unknown," or "Unexplored." Mysterious lands—why had no one investigated them, he wondered.

Lincoln believed that his father, of all his achievements, was proudest of his part in the triumphal outcome after many near disasters of the Columbian Exposition in Chicago in 1893. While he reluctantly accepted his appointment to head it, he plunged at once into getting it under way. He had the vision to engage the architect Daniel H. Burnham as the fair's designer and Frederick Law Olmsted, architect of New York's Central Park, to cooperate with Burnham in laying out the grounds. When the exposition coffers at one point were near exhaustion, Ellsworth advanced $800,000 of his own money. The fair was a success as Ellsworth never doubted it would be. Gate receipts met all deficits, even returning a profit.

For Lincoln and Clare the exposition (their father never called it a fair) was an endless lark. With passes to everything, they missed none of the attractions. At dinner at home they met the visiting great—Paderewski, who came several times and always played for them, the poet and journalist Eugene Field, and such artists as George Inness.

Although aware of the love and unfailing provision for him, the son confessed in his autobiography that he never felt close to his father, that he could not break through his reserve. Lincoln was not alone in this. Few indeed saw the gentler side of James Ellsworth. His daughter Clare did and likewise his second wife, the former Mrs. Julia Clark Finck of Chicago.

Despite demands of his far-flung interests, no details escaped him. He noticed a well-cared-for flower garden at the shaft head of one of his mines. Such evidence of devotion to beauty won him, and on enquiry he learned it was the work of an English miner, Harry Cooper. Before long Cooper gave up mining to take over gardening at Evamere, with his family installed in a nearby house provided by his employer. As a side interest, Cooper built a greenhouse in his backyard, raising there out-of-season vegetables and flowers.

In his forties during the last decade of the nineteenth century,

Ellsworth, president of an important Chicago bank, builder of one of the city's first skyscrapers, and operator of coal mines in three states, was a national figure. The stern man who thirty years before had been marketing his farmer-father's hogs, now was reputedly a millionaire. And he was embarked on another venture: development in the most up-to-date procedure of 16,000 acres of coal lands in Washington County Pennsylvania. He organized a fleet of ships to carry his coal to European ports whose harbors he had personally inspected. Within the Pennsylvania acreage he laid out a model village that he called Ellsworth, putting up attractive, substantial houses for the miners, schools for their children, stores with good quality, low priced wares. Despite his fanatic temperance convictions, he acquiesced to his workmen and set up a tavern where beer was obtainable—at certain hours—but no hard liquor. He was adamantly opposed to unions, feeling he could do more for his men than any labor organization. Nonetheless union organizers infiltrated the area and, to his keen disappointment, won over the miners. In legislation under the administration of President Theodore Roosevelt, whom he heartily disliked, private freight cars were to be largely prohibited. With the odds he saw stacked against him, in 1907 Ellsworth sold his Pennsylvania holdings, and, between trips to his Florentine Villa Palmieri, stopped off at Evamere.

The academy, he learned in the meantime, was in trouble: the small subsidy received from Western Reserve College since its move to Cleveland was to be discontinued. Ellsworth was appealed to for help. An endowment of $100,000, it was estimated by the school's head, would save it. Ellsworth agreed to supply half that amount if the school raised the other half. Despite the officials' superhuman efforts, not anywhere near that amount was forthcoming in pledges and Western Reserve Academy closed its doors in 1903.

In the words of Lucien Price, "Campus walks grew up to weeds. Dormitories tumbled to decay. Roofs leaked and shutters banged. Plaster fell in and panes fell out. No haunted house was ever half so dismal. For these buildings were haunted by the departed spirits of youth."

This was the scene that met James Ellsworth's eyes when he returned to Hudson in 1907 after selling off his Pennsylvania properties. In typical fashion he determined to revitalize both the academy and the village. And over a period of years he did so. He gave the village modern electric light, water, and sewage plants. He converted an old cheese warehouse into a social clubhouse for the village and began planting trees. In turn the village voted out the saloons, placed its electric wires underground, and planted more trees, mostly elms.

In 1912, James Ellsworth and the former trustees of the academy regained control of the property. South College had been torn down in 1884, and the old Middle College was now razed and Seymour Hall erected on its site. The other buildings were renovated, the hedge planted, and general improvements instituted all over the campus. With a $200,000 endowment fund and a total value of $500,000, Western Reserve Academy reopened its doors in September 1916.

Hudson's benefactor spent his winters in Florence, at the Villa Palmieri, and his summers in Hudson. In May 1925 his son, Lincoln, with members of the Amundsen polar expedition, disappeared into the arctic wastes. They were lost for twenty-five days. Finding their way out to Kings Bay on June 18, they learned that James Ellsworth had died of pneumonia sixteen days earlier at the Villa Palmieri at the age of seventy-six.

His body was returned to Hudson for burial. The funeral services in Western Reserve Academy Chapel, conducted by the Reverend Clarence S. Gee, pastor of the Congregational church, were described in the local newspaper:

> The funeral services held for the late James W. Ellsworth last Thursday morning, were beautiful in their simplicity, thus carrying out the principles he practiced thruout his life. The great oaken casket was covered with a beautiful blanket of red roses and maidenhair ferns and about the casket and on the walls hung great wreaths and garlands of flowers the gifts of friends from all over the country.
>
> The old historic chapel, which he had rescued from decay, made a beautiful setting for these services when his relatives, business associates and friends met to pay their last homage to the man whose generosity and good will has made our village one of the choice suburbs of this section, and whose prominence as a financier and philanthropist has brought national prominence to his birthplace.

The village of Hudson and Western Reserve Academy owe much to this rich, powerful, aloof, perhaps lonely, man. And while there have been many men and women whose lives have enriched Hudson and its school and there will be more to come, it seems fitting to end this tale that began with David Hudson with the passing of James Ellsworth.

ROBERT AND JON IZANT
on the Congregational church steps.

North Main Street, Hudson, Ohio.

EPILOGUE

OUR STURDY MODEL T, with its brass headlights well shined for the momentous journey, had transported us from Cleveland to the top of Hines Hill. Before us the road stretched in a sure straight course to Hudson and our new home in the village. We slowed the motor to savor the scene. Surely, we thought, it must have been the same with those other adventuring settlers in the last century when their heavy-footed oxen had brought their wagons to this same hill, and the pioneers had their first glimpse of the strange promiseful wilderness that lay ahead.

It was fall 1924. James W. Ellsworth would die within the year, leaving behind him the legacy of his "model town," Hudson.

We arrived on Halloween, a few days before Calvin Coolidge and his running mate Charles G. Dawes won the national election. It was the middle of the "Incredible Twenties," the age of Jazz and Prohibition, of bathtub gin and speakeasies, of Marathon Dances and Mah-jongg. Women's fashions called for hip-low waistlines and skirts that dipped gracelessly in the rear. Radios, improved over the early crystal sets, appeared in more and more homes and talkies were soon to take the place of the silent movies.

Oil, as much talked about then as now, saturated the news; Senator Thomas J. Walsh had begun the probe of Teapot Dome oil leases in 1923, and shortly the investigations led to criminal prosecutions. Newspapers headlined hooch hounds' gun battles with bootleggers. Controversy raged through the decade over the death sentence judgment for the Sacco-Vanzetti pair, and the Pharoah's ancient curse hovered over the opening of King Tut's fabulous tomb in 1922. Galsworthy issued *The White Monkey* (1924) in his popular Forsyte Saga series, and Sinclair Lewis's *Main Street* (1920) and *Babbitt* (1922) were discussed by everyone, even by those who had not read the books. Mencken's *American Mercury* (begun in 1924) was to become the status symbol of the intelligentsia. Everybody sang "Yes, We Have No Bananas," learned the Charleston, and worried about inflation's runaway prices.

Characteristic of the booming economy, our rent in Cleveland was escalating with no ceiling in sight. Besides, we both came from families who thought it practically immoral to waste money on rent. And it so happened that my husband, Robert Izant, had fallen in love with Hudson years before in his senior year at Western Reserve University. At that time, he had been in charge of the annual relay race held between the University and Western Reserve Academy at the original campus in Hudson.

Much had happened to him in the interval since college, including the Argonne battles six years before in the "war to end all wars." Somehow he had tucked away in a corner of his mind the memory of the peaceful village and now was reviving it. The quiet Hudson

hinterland would be a good place in which to rear his boys—Bob was three and Jon a year and a half. And, with what seemed then a long look into the future, their father added that when they were old enough the children could attend the academy! He would get to his bank in downtown Cleveland via the Pennsylvania Railroad. There were twelve trains a day, each way, for Cleveland commuters. All stopped in Hudson, a change point on the main line to New York and Pittsburgh, with a spur to Orrville for connection to Chicago and a convenient "doodle bug" shuttle back and forth to Akron. A test ride demonstrated that the train provided quicker and more comfortable transportation than his present city bus trips. And for less money. The railroad's monthly ticket, good for 40 rides, cost $8.75. Later, I was to find the train most convenient for the wives, too. We could leave for Cleveland at ten in the morning after the children had gone to school, and return on the 4:10. It gave ample time to prepare dinner and drive back to the station to pick up our husbands arriving on the 6:15.

South of the main station, a smaller one for the Akron passenger and freight traffic was in the charge of a good looking and obviously very capable woman in her late forties, maybe, named Anna Lee. To our amazement, we discovered she was the great-great-granddaughter of David Hudson! She was very proud of the fact and also that she lived in the Hudson House on North Main Street, the first frame dwelling in the township.

The house we bought was on College Street. It was built in the 1870s and looked it, architecturally speaking. Later, when the village took on city ways and numbered its houses, we drew 69. College Street was unpaved, muting the usual street clatter. We appreciated the lovely quiet after living on Euclid Avenue with its busy traffic and clanging streetcars. Our boys looked on the roadway as a wonderful playground, especially made for them, and scampered out to dig in the soft dirt whenever they could elude their elders.

The only real estate dealer in town, Weldon Wood, handled the sale. He was president of the local Western Reserve Telephone Company which he founded in 1910, amalgamating several small lines. He pointed out proudly that the Hudson scene was not marred by

unsightly telegraph poles and strings of overhead power lines; underground conduits carried the wires. All this was due to his friend Mr. James Ellsworth, he indicated, not mentioning what we later learned had been his own important role in the undertaking.

Mr. Wood could take care of our insurance, he suggested. He urged us to take advantage of the Hudson Club, housed in the pillared building (now the academy's Hayden Hall) diagonally across from our house. It was given to the town by Mr. Ellsworth and was for everyone in the community, he said. Of course, our new friend opined, we would want a telephone. He would see to our having one, which he did, the day we moved in. The owner of our property was Mrs. Harlan N. Wood (no relation to Weldon Wood) whose father Bristol had built the house. White haired, plump, and jolly, she was almost twenty years older than her husband, a highly regarded master, soon appointed the academy's dean and always "Dean" to us. He impressed one at once—slim, perfectly groomed, a proper New Englander with a gentle sense of

President's house, built in 1830. The two wooden wings were removed in 1914.

humor showing through his reticence. We learned—but not from him—that he was president of the bank, trustee of the library, and an important official of the Congregational church. He volunteered to introduce us at the bank, hoped we would make full use of the library, and invited us some Sunday to attend church with him and Mrs. Wood.

The Woods lived on campus, in half of the double house. It was known as the President's House because early college heads had occupied it, they explained. On one of our first look-see tours of Hudson, we had admired that fine old brick with its pair of identical classic doorways and elliptical fanlights. It was at the north end of College Street where a double row of lofty elms arched over the roadway, giant trees that long since have succumbed to a devastating disease.

The Izant house at 69 College Street.

When we first were shown "our" house, we noticed in the entrance hall its only window, small and high-placed, and painted over with a strange, gaudy design that effectively kept out the little light it might have admitted. I wondered, out loud unfortunately, how soon I could get rid of that—if we should buy the house. Dean Wood, who had heard every word, commented quietly, "My wife painted that when she was a girl."

Downstairs ceilings were high, the wallpaper a lugubrious pattern of black and tan leaves and vines. It did nothing for the woodwork, a "natural yellow," varnished to a shiny glow. But the rooms were big with a comfortable feel about them. We were young and optimistic and very happy, the four of us in this our first very own home. And my husband promised that when we could afford it, we would have new wallpaper and the woodwork painted white.

Sledding on the Hudson Street hill.

The Dean's wife came to call. She was sweet and friendly and it was easy to see why she had been a village belle in her youth, as we learned later. She had grown up in the house and loved to come back to it, she said. Leading me into the front room, which she termed the parlor, she pointed out where she and the Dean had stood when they were married. Over there was where her grand piano stood. (We didn't have a piano yet.) In their courting days, she had "accompanied Harlan, who loved to sing, and still does," she added. In the course of this cozy tête-à-tête, I was led to confide in her our dreams of new paper and white paint—when we could afford it.

I thought she would be pleased at such plans for her old home. She was not. "That woodwork is matched sycamore," she exclaimed

Walking to lunch at Cutler Hall.

indignantly. "My father personally selected every piece and was very proud of it. He was an expert on wood. Why in the world would anyone want to paint it?"

The strangest feature of our home was its arrangement of water faucets—three of them at every outlet—at the kitchen sink, in the bathroom at the washbasin and bathtub, and in the laundry. One supplied cold water, one hot, and the third rain water from the cistern under our dining room window. (Our first project was to have a rock rolled onto the cover lest two curious little boys might want to investigate the cistern's depths.) The cold water, we were informed, was pumped from deep artesian wells, part of Mr. Ellsworth's contribution to the community. It was pure, delicious, and cold, even in summer. And hard. It repelled soap and any

discoverable washing powder. A shampoo in it was a disaster. Clothes washed in it came out stiff and no cleaner than when immersed. Village fathers refused to contaminate this excellent water with any kind of softener. We soon were hoarding every drop of rainwater, hoping each shower would continue all day, and turn into a cloudburst!

Another challenge, to me at least, was coping with our oil stove. There was no gas in the village and electric stoves were new and rare. Our oil stove was an especially fine model, complete with oven, the gift of my kind mother-in-law who had tried to dissuade us from moving to this benighted place, but since we had, wanted to help ease our way as much as possible. I never have had a better performing oven, but I often forgot to fill the oil reservoir and the wicks frequently smoked because they needed trimming. Our house, like every house in town, gave off a subtle aroma of kerosene the moment you stepped inside.

The old Congregational church rectory, *left*, and Club House, *above*.

For our first Hudson Thanksgiving, coming on the heels of our arrival, we invited our Cleveland families for dinner at the Club House. Diggs, presiding as both chef and club manager, was capable and gracious. He served a delicious meal, the whole experience going a long way in reconciling our city relatives to our move "to the country."

With the first snowfall, we were startled to see a horse approaching on the sidewalk. It was pulling a triangular wooden contraption on which the driver balanced himself expertly. Two little boys sat at his feet, obviously enjoying the ride. George Gannon, whose title might have been "Keeper of the Walks," was at his job. Until Mr. Ellsworth installed electric lights, we were told Mr. Gannon had been the town lamplighter, going about in a two-wheeled cart behind this same horse. After him, sidewalk maintenance was taken over in the same way by C. H. "Duff" Billiter, who doubled as constable and was our entire police force. Never have our sidewalks been as well cared for as by these two men and their horses.

Louella Dodds on the fine sandstone walks of Church Street.

Along this part of College Street, the walks were expertly laid sandstone, but in numerous places the old wooden sidewalks remained. They were hazardous with loose boards that flew up and hit anyone making a misstep. They were an anathema to baby carriages or strollers. A couple of young mothers, newcomers to the village, drew up a petition to have flagging replace the relics. I presented a copy for signature to our neighbor, Miss Caroline Ellsworth, a relative of *the* Mr. Ellsworth as were all the numerous residents of that name. Miss Ellsworth, later Mrs. Grant Blackburn, lived in a little white house behind a white picket fence on Aurora Street next to the Congregational church. The walk passing her place was one of the worst in town. (The house has been moved since to 189 Aurora Street to make way for an addition to the church.) "I certainly will not sign your paper," she said tartly. "We

Caroline Ellsworth's little house.

have had wooden walks since I was a girl. They're better for you than flagging—don't jar the spine so much. If you like stone walks, why don't you stay in the city where you had them?"

In our new life, Weldon Wood's telephone system was an experience in itself. Our phone was installed by Raymond Pettingell. His grandfather, William Pettingell, had served as treasurer of the college for many years. He had come from London where he and his partner were tailors to George IV, and William's mother and wife were "staymakers" and "stayfitters" to Victoria as princess and queen.

The telephone exchange functioned on the second floor of the bank building. Its chief and, for a while, sole operator was Annie Cameron. As our phone number, we were assigned 175—no exchange, merely the three digits. The figure represented the company's 175th hook-up.

Subscribers, however, had little need of telephone numbers or even of a directory when Annie was on the board. You merely lifted the receiver and told her you would like to talk to Mrs. Jones. From her high perch above the busy corner of Main and Aurora streets, Annie surveyed all Hudson's comings and goings. She would inform you she had just seen Mrs. Jones—she would probably refer to her as "Mary" Jones—go into one of the stores. Annie said she would ring you when Mrs. Jones had returned home. And she kept her word.

Annie reigned by night as well as by day. A popular topic at social gatherings was to conjecture how Annie got any sleep. Actually, the management (meaning Weldon Wood) had installed a couch for her convenience. And Annie took advantage of it, as was realized by every subscriber who tried to rouse her to put through a call in the wee hours. But no one ever thought of complaining if she over-dozed now and again. Annie was too good to lose.

Mr. Wood would be amazed at how his grandsons, the Case brothers, have developed his little company. Weldon Case is chairman and chief executive of Alltel Corporation, the nation's fifth largest independent telephone system. One unit is the Western Reserve Telephone Company, greatly extended and headed by Weldon's brother, Nelson Henry Case. They operate from a spacious headquarters building in Hudson's new Executive Park, a 158-acre landscaped enclave on Boston Mills Road. A park brochure stresses the advantages of living in Hudson, described as "a prestige community that reflects the cultural influences of the first settlers who came from Connecticut."

The Cases are conscious of this inheritance. Their line, through their late father, Harry Case, reaches to Chauncey Case, a Connecticut native who purchased a large tract of land in Hudson

Henry Barlow, Clara May Barlow, and Grandma (Mrs. Henry) Case.

in 1814. The Case homestead on Barlow Road was built in 1826 of bricks fired on the place and was one of the first brick houses in the Reserve. It is occupied by Donald C. Barlow and family; Mr. Barlow also is descended from Chauncey Case and, until recently, operated the original Case farm, which, though diminished in acreage from the frontier era, was one of the last working farms hereabouts. Allotments now, with row on row of new houses, are crowding close to it.

The post office was on Main Street in quarters once the grocery store of Patrick Moran who owned the building. Mrs. Mae Crane was the postmistress with Edna Robinson her assistant. Since we had to go for our mail, we met all our friends daily in the post office lobby. It was a great way to keep up with village news, not to say gossip! A lot of sociability was lost when Hudson became citified and instituted home delivery.

The Frederick Baldwin house as it appeared in 1924, just prior to its purchase by the HLHS.

The Hudson Library and Historical Society had recently moved into a delightful old house facing the green at the corner of East Main and Aurora streets. Harlan Wood and his wife invited us to the formal opening on New Year's Day, 1925. The house had been the birthplace (1841) of Caroline Baldwin Babcock who founded the library in 1910. At her death in 1921, she left $100,000 in trust for the library. Funds were earmarked also for a perpetual free lecture series that the library was to administer. Mrs. Babcock's gift was to be known as the Baldwin-Babcock Memorial, honoring her parents and her late husband, Perry H. Babcock, a well-to-do Cleveland businessman.

She had expressed the wish that the library, then occupying temporary space in the Club House, might someday be housed in one of Hudson's old homes. The house where she was born, no longer a family property, was purchased, renovated, and readied for its new use for $12,016.27. Built by Mrs. Baldwin's father in the 1830s, the house may have been the work of carpenter-joiners hired during construction of the college buildings. Mrs. Babcock was a historian at heart and, loyal to her pioneer ancestry, indicated that the historical, as pertaining to Hudson, was to be as much stressed as the library in the future society. "I would have over the door," she stipulated, "the names of the six men who founded the village, the church and the college." On New Year's Day, there was a formal dedication of a bronze plaque above the entrance that did homage to:

David Hudson	Benjamin Oviatt
Birdsey Norton	Theodore Parmele
Nathaniel Norton	Stephen Baldwin

The last listed was Mrs. Babcock's grandfather. Only one of the six, David Hudson, visited the Ohio lands he bought; however, children of all the others settled here. There were numerous intermarriages. Consequently, a number of Hudsonites today claim more than one of the six as ancestors, and great are their genealogical complications!

The society's home, Mrs. Babcock hoped, "Would be a center of community and social life." And we found it exactly that. Villagers met there for friendly, spirited discussions on family living patterns, the "new" education, local issues, or perhaps the review of a controversial book. The leader often was Ralph Boothby, the stimulating and friendly new headmaster of Western Reserve Academy. He had come in June 1924 from Cleveland where we had known him and his program as director of the progressive Park School. At some library gatherings, residents exhibited their collections, maybe a rare early Ohio glass, or precious Hudson artifacts, often with owners giving informative talks about their treasures. Someone was sure to bring cookies or cake and somebody else provided coffee. So many came that often we had to sit on the stairs. The house was small but charming, with a warm, welcoming air about it.

The Library and Historical Society headquarters, now big and efficient, has expanded twice since those days. Yet it has kept Mrs. Babcock's birthplace practically unchanged. She would be pleased at the increasing emphasis on Hudson history, with the librarian also a curator and full-time archivist overseeing a growing body of original pioneer documents. A valuable recent acquisition is the collection of David Hudson papers now on microfilm for easy viewing by researchers.

BOB AND JON IZANT,
HAROLD TURNER.

Our next door neighbor, Donald Turner, was descended from Theodore Parmele, one of the "Founding Six." The Turners had two little boys, Donald and Harold, the same age as ours, providing them with ready-made and very welcome playmates. Mr. Turner operated a newsstand and cigar store on Main Street, where he also sold penny candy, including long rubbery strings of licorice.

Midway back, his store was divided by a glass partition to make an office for J. M. Darling, veteran justice of the peace and notary public. In cold weather Justice Darling kept his potbellied stove fired to a glow, making his little room a cheery rendezvous for his cronies, the town's elder statesmen. In the comfortable old chairs provided, they smoked their pipes and decried the changes overtaking Hudson, or played Pedro and Civil War High Five.

Mr. Turner's father, Charles, and another son, Francis, ran the mill—Turner's Mill when it *was* a mill. We bought coal for our furnace from them, oil for our cookstove, 50-pound sacks of flour—there was

a big built-in flour bin in our kitchen. Francis had a pampered
female cat that he catered to with special delicacies. And well he
might, for he declared that with her around, no mouse or rat dared
so much as sniff at the stores of grain and feed kept on hand for
the many local farmers. The cat regularly presented the miller with
a batch of kittens that were welcomed as "Mother's Little Helpers"
and turned loose to romp about the mill. Now and then the offspring
became too numerous even for kindhearted Francis, and he would
give one or two away to children coming to the mill with their
unwary parents. A Turner cat was a pet in many a Hudson home,
including ours.

The old Buss store, built by the Baldwin family in 1842.

Retail shopping was confined to the west side of Main Street,
beginning with the Buss Store at the south end (site of today's
Hudson Square Building). It was a cavernous place of three floors,

originally stocked for an exclusively agricultural clientele, and now
too big and unadjusted to a changing village-oriented community.
The proprietor, Freddie Buss, an affable little man, represented the
third generation in the business. It was established by his
grandfather, John Buss, an Englishman who in 1833 came to Hudson
as a young man to attend the college. His plans to study for the
ministry were given up because of ill health, and he clerked in a
couple of local stores until opening his own big establishment. After
his death in 1879, his son Charles, who also attended the college,
carried on. Farmers drove in from miles around to trade in kind
with produce and in turn pick up a plow or a needed piece of harness
and maybe a few yards of dress material for the women at home.
They tied their teams out in front and, when we came, the hitching
posts still stood at the curb.

Fred's sister Gussie, quick-moving and bird-like, was as short as
her brother, but more concerned than he about dwindling revenues.
She presided in a mezzanine floor office as cashier. Through her
thick-lensed spectacles, she surveyed the downstairs sales room and
missed very little of what went on. She received the cash from
transactions via whizzing overhead trolley and, after carefully
counting the change, dispatched it down to her brother by the same
noisy apparatus.

D. J. Joyce had a grocery nearby. He and Charles Buss, feuding
through the years, had built large houses side by side on Church
Street, each having tried to outdo the other in size of dwelling. Mr.
Joyce dispensed his wares in bulk—crisp soda crackers and spicy
gingersnaps in candy-striped paper bags, sugar by the pound, and
coffee ground-to-order on a big, hand-operated mill. Butter was
scooped from a crockful freshly churned by a township farmer who
also supplied eggs.

Storekeeper Joyce greeted customers with effusive Irish affability—until he discovered they were also patronizing rival Main Street grocers. Then his manner cooled to chilliness, a sales technique that did not encourage customers' return to his store.

Nearby, in narrow quarters, George Gott opened the "Biggest Little Hardware Store in the World." From his crowded shelves and drawers, tiered ceiling-high, he could extricate just the hinge or screw you sought. Beside him in an equally small space, David Vogel manned a barber shop. It was a busy place, seldom without customers waiting for hair cuts at 25 cents a head. At the north end of Main Street, Peter MacGregor operated a tailor shop, carrying on a trade he mastered as a youth in his native Scotland. After the Great War, as he always referred to World War I, he and his wife

found their way to Hudson. Soon the best dressed men in the village were wearing MacGregor outfits—perfect fit and expensive. You could recognize the suits at a glance.

We had one store that was exclusively a butcher shop—sawdust floor, meat cut and weighed while you waited—or delivered if you ordered by 'phone. It was S. E. Sawyer's. Few knew what his real name was—he was "Dick" to everyone, and a gentleman. It is said he got diverted somehow into the meat trade, and never really enjoyed it. No matter. He wore his long white apron with professional distinction and carved his steaks with the hand of a master. We called him the Bride's Friend. If an inexperienced young matron courageously decided to serve a crowned roast—with paper frills—for company, she knew she could count on Dick Sawyer for directions about cooking it and making the gravy.

Above the butcher shop, reached by a long, steep stairway, Kate Hild had her millinery shop, a busy place where she employed a couple of helpers. They made dresses as well as hats. Miss Hild was a member of the H.U.B. club. Reports of its meetings appeared frequently in the local news sheet but it was some time before we learned what the mysterious initials stood for: Hudson's Unclaimed Blessings. It was an exclusive, merry group of the village's most prominent spinsters.

The only business that has survived since the mid-twenties is Saywell's Drug Store—same name, same location at 160 Main Street. Fred Saywell opened it in 1909, two years before Dick Sawyer began business. We patronized Fred for drug needs and also for his soda fountain. On summer evenings in the days when everybody knew everybody, neighbors gathered at Saywell's and climbed upon the high, revolving stools to order an after-dinner nut sundae or maybe a banana split—prohibition day indulgences before the weight watching era. After December 1933 when liquor became legal and respectable again, the druggist procured a liquor license, and we went to his place for more than drugs and chocolate sundaes.

As we strolled along Aurora Street on the way to the drug store, we passed the Park Hotel that faces the green near the corner of Main Street. Pat and Minnie Moran, the hotel's owners, and Rita Camp, their indispensable majordomo, were sure to be rocking side-by-side on the front porch enjoying the summer evening calm, and we invariably stopped for a chat. Rita was black and the friend of everyone, especially of the sick and of little girls for whom she made lovely doll dresses.

The hotel is one of Hudson's most noteworthy buildings, "that stupendous Gothic pile . . . so unlike anything else in the village," in the words of the architectural historian Eric Johannesen.

One day, a handsome, gangling boy knocked at our door. "I came over to see if you'd rent half of your garage to me. I'd pay a dollar a month." He was Johnnie Morse who lived a few doors away on Aurora Street. His father, it appeared, had ordered him and his "clutter" out of the family basement workshop.

JOHN MORSE

"I've got to have a place for my photography and my machines," the six-foot teen-ager blurted out.

We had two boys, and their father was sympathetic. He concluded the deal agreeing not to ask for the rent in advance. Shortly, John Morse, Sr. called on us. "You'll rue the day you ever let Johnnie in," he warned. But we kept to our contract.

What Johnnie called his "ideas" have netted him drawersful of patent records—one hundred, maybe twice that many. He hasn't bothered to count them. Ideas, it appears, have always been dancing around in his head. He wanted our garage so he could try out some of them. He moved in at once, bringing a miscellaneous lot of tools, remnants of cameras, knocked-down engines, auto parts—and his battered motorcycle. His collection grew daily. It attracted our boys and every boy—and some girls—in the neighborhood. Johnnie was pleasant and patient with them, and they adored him. Soon we parked our car in the driveway, left our lawn mower and garden rakes under a tree.

Johnnie hammered and sawed noisily and happily, often late into the night. Then he would crank up his motorcycle and zoom off, waking everyone in our house and the people on both sides of us. After repeated complaints from our neighbors, we consulted John, Sr. He washed his hands of the whole affair with an amused, "I told you so." This was the first shop acquired by John F. Morse, Jr., genius inventor, who organized Hudson's multi-million dollar Morse Controls, Division of Incom International. His plant has overflowed from a string of shops on Clinton Street to what used to be the ballpark. The village opened a public highway, Morse Road, to help handle the factory traffic. Mr. Morse is world-famous, gray-haired, and a grandfather. But he's still Johnnie Morse to Hudson, and he would not want it otherwise. We call him, proudly, "Hudson's Edison."

Since those friendly, bucolic days in the twenties, James Ellsworth's "model town" has forged ahead. The reinvigorated Western Reserve Academy is known nationwide, its high standards of scholarship fulfilling the promise of the early college.

Wouldn't it be wonderful if David Hudson could come back for just a day to see all that has happened to the tiny settlement in the wilderness that bears his name?

NOTES TO TEXT
AND ILLUSTRATIONS

PREFACE

The illustration at the head of the Publisher's Preface is of the Hudson village
green circa 1900, before James Ellsworth had the power lines placed
underground. The photograph at the head of the Acknowledgments is of the
drive leading to Great Elm, the author's longtime Hudson home, named for
the Izant ancestral home in England.

The book's designer would like to acknowledge the artistic contributions of Avis
and Mark Andres, the Guldan family, and Marjorie Cain.

. . . AS THE LAST BRITISH TROOPS WERE PUTTING OUT TO SEA . . .

Hudson-Norton wedding: Goshen Congregational Church records, 1800, Vol. I.
Hudson later was "contaminated" by the philosophies of the French Revolution
but at the time of his marriage was listed in good standing. Anna and Nathaniel
were born in 1760, David in 1761, and Birdsey in 1763. Anna's father, David
Norton, who died five years before her marriage, was a brother of Ebenezer,
Birdsey's and Nathaniel's father. Anna's mother, left with nine young children,
lived in the family home on Pie Hill.

The Reverend A. G. Hibbard, *History of the Town of Goshen, Connecticut*
(1897), pp. 516, 508, 616. This book, based on Goshen records and genealogies
collected by Deacon Lewis Mills Norton, Birdsey's nephew, is a valuable source
of information on early Goshen, homeland of many Hudson, Ohio settlers. After
a lifetime in the family cheese business, the Deacon gave his time to collecting
this lore, poring over old documents and faded letters, and studying worn
gravestones. Being a Norton all doors were open to him. He was a familiar
figure as he traveled about the countryside in an old-style buggy behind a fat
little mare who, his friends said, stopped at every Norton home and turned
into every cemetery.

We are indebted to the Deacon for such tidbits as the origin of Birdsey
Norton's unusual first name (unfortunately often misspelled "Birdseye"). It
came, we are told, from his grandmother Dinah Birdsey, who as the personable
Widow Beach married his grandfather Samuel Norton. It has reappeared
through the years and is a patronymic today, testimony to the prominence of
the original Birdsey Norton.

The Deacon assembled his collection in two large volumes, each of six hundred
handwritten, legible pages. This magnum opus, although forgotten for many

years, fortunately was well preserved. The two volumes are now in the
Connecticut State Library in Hartford, part of the Barbour Collection. Hibbard
incorporated much of it practically verbatim in his history with full
acknowledgment to the Deacon.

Wedding attire: Alice Earle, *Customs and Fashions in Old New England* (1893);
Peter Copeland, *Working Dress in Colonial and Revolutionary America* (1977).
Congregational church austerity frowned on luxuries like heat in churches as
well as all forms of elaborate dress. David M. Roth, *Connecticut* (1979), pp.
34–65.

Washington's farewell to his officers, Fraunces Tavern, December 4, 1783: Henry
Cabot Lodge, *George Washington* (1924), Vol. I, pp. 345–46.

Washington appears before Congress, December 23, 1783 to resign as commander-in-
chief: Lodge, Vol. I, p. 347; *We, the People, the story of the United States
Capitol, published by the United States Historical Society* (1978), p. 79.

David Hudson senior purchases land in Goshen 1765, builds three-story house, known
as the Hudson House: Hibbard, p. 60; home of David and Anna and family
until their departure for Ohio; Goshen Congregational church records, 1800,
Vol. I; Goshen Town Hall records.

Old-time pillion horseback travel for women, uncomfortable and often precarious,
persisted especially as part of wedding rituals: Hibbard, p. 177, probably a
Deacon Norton contribution.

Christmas Eve celebration at Mount Vernon: Lodge, Vol. II, p. 1.

The photographs on page 4 of Nashapaug Pond and on page 5 of the house David
Hudson was born in (as it appeared in 1934) are from the Grace Goulder Izant
collection now with the Hudson Library and Historical Society (HLHS). The
photograph on page 7 of the chapel of the Western Reserve Academy was taken
by Grace Goulder Izant and is now in the HLHS.

THE FATHER OF THE WESTERN RESERVE

The portrait of Roger Sherman on page 8 is by Ralph Earl. Courtesy of the Yale
University Art Gallery.

The Northwest Territory: Emelius O. Randall and Daniel J. Ryan, *History of Ohio*
(1912), Vol. II, p. 412. Expressing the negative point of view about the newly
acquired domain, James Madison wrote to Jefferson: "A great part of the
territory is miserably poor, especially that near Lakes Erie and Michigan, and
that upon which the Mississippi and the Missouri and the Illinois consists of
extensive plans which have not had from appearances, and will not have, a
single bush on them for years." Walter Havighust, *The Heartland* (1926), p. 86.

Connecticut's grant from King Charles II: Randall and Ryan, p. 576.

Speculation in territorial lands: Frederick Merk, *History of the Western Movement*
(1978), p. 104; Cecil B. Currey, *Code Number 72/ Benjamin Franklin, Patriot
or Spy?* (1965), pp. 59 ff., 294.

David Hudson adds to his farm: Goshen Town Hall records.

Virginia's Ohio lands: Known as the Virginia Military District, it lay between the Little Miami and Scioto rivers. Among prominent Virginia veterans receiving allotments in the tract were Generals Washington, George Rogers Clark, and Daniel Morgan. Washington's portion of 3,051 acres was in what became Clermont County. Joseph T. Ferguson, *Ohio Land Grants*, n.d., probably about 1969, p. 3.

The Charter Oak: The original oak, after standing for almost three hundred years, was reduced to a stump in an 1893 hurricane. But the charter evidently was saved, for it is safely housed today in the Connecticut State Library at Hartford, Connecticut. Ferguson, pp. 7, 14–15; *Connecticut, a Guide to its Roads and Lore* (1938), pp. 170, 181.

The Continental Congress also was confronted with a population of squatters in Transappalachia. A mixed lot made up of veterans of the bitter Indian wars and gun-happy, irresponsible drifters had taken over frontier areas without regard to land titles. The Indians, too, were becoming increasingly resentful of the growing white invasion of tribal lands. Merk, p. 98 ff.; Eugene H. Roseboom and Francis P. Weisenburger, *A History of Ohio* (1967), pp. 43, 51.

Wyoming Settlements: Christopher Collier, *Connecticut in the Continental Congress* (1976), p. 50 ff. This scholarly pamphlet contributes many heretofore little-known details about the creation of the Western Reserve and is the basis for much of this chapter.

William Penn grants: King Charles II to discharge a debt of 16,000 pounds owed to wealthy Admiral Penn gave the land that became Pennsylvania to his son, the handsome William Penn. The latter was said to have been a disappointment to the admiral because of his espousal of the Quaker faith. Young Penn had thought to call the area Sylvania, but the king so admired the sword-carrying Quaker that he named it Pennsylvania. Thus it became the only American colony that carried the name of its founder. Antonia Fraser, *Royal Charles* (1979), p. 433; William Wister Comfort, *William Penn* (1944), pp. 33, 173; James Truslow Adams, ed., *Album of American History* (1944), p. 228.

The Wyoming holocaust: Well might Connecticut decry the tragedy; it ranks as one of the blackest episodes in early American annals. Harlan Hatcher, *The Western Reserve* (1949), pp. 18–20; Merk, p. 90.

Roger Sherman: Born in Massachusetts, Sherman settled early in Connecticut and began his career as a shoemaker. Self-educated, he could be seen at his bench with an open book before him, maybe a volume of Milton, Pope, or Dryden. He studied surveying and law and acquired extensive land. Moving to New Haven he became its first mayor and contributed to Yale's first chapel. He served as treasurer of Yale and was given an honorary degree. Collier; *The New England Quarterly*, Vol. 5, (1932), pp. 221 ff.; L. H. Bontell, *Life of Roger Sherman* (1896); *Yale Law Journal* (1908–32), pp. 21–36. The Reverend Jonathan Edwards, Jr., Pastor, New Haven Congregational Church, delivered a eulogy at Sherman's funeral, 1793. Copy in Western Reserve Historical Society,

Cleveland, Ohio (hereafter referred to as WRHS) covers twenty-four pages.

Gertrude of Wyoming: Van Dyke Brooks, *The World of Washington Irving* (1945), pp. 110 ff., 172.

The Reverend Josiah Sherman was criticized because of his sermons, his pompous bearing, and his attitude toward those who differed with him. "He was," in short, "not unconscious of his mental superiority to those to whom he ministered." Hibbard, pp. 86, 88, 307.

LAND FEVER AND THREE WIVES

The illustration on page 17 is of Branford, Connecticut, and is taken from an old woodcut by John Warner Barber.

The Ordinance of 1787 was the outgrowth of the Ordinance of 1785 in which Jefferson had had a hand. This earlier ordinance has been called "one of the most important and admirable measures ever passed by an American legislature." Merk, p. 102 ff.; Beverly W. Bond, *The Foundations of Ohio*, vol. I of *The History of the State of Ohio*, ed. Carl Wittke, (1941), p. 258 ff.

Land speculators: Merk, p. 79 ff.

"The Yankee exodus into all parts of the American West" was "the most influential movement our country has known": Stewart H. Holbrook, *The Yankee Exodus* (1950), p. 10.

The Ohio Company of Associates: Roseboom and Weisenburger, pp. 47–49; Merk, p. 104 ff.; Grace Goulder, *This is Ohio* (1965), p. 17 ff.

The first Nortons in America: *Steiner's History of Guilford* (1897), p. 139 ff.

The Hudsons and Nortons in Goshen: Deacon Lewis Norton's notes as found in Hibbard, pp. 184, 365, 370, 516.

Cheese-making: Hibbard, p. 165. The fine flavor of the local cheese was due to a pasture grass known as hardback. Hibbard, p. 49.

The China trade: As early as the 1790s, Connecticut ships were in the South Seas picking up pearls and sandalwood that the skippers traded for tea and other luxuries enjoyed by wealthy colonials. The towns on Long Island Sound like Stonington and New Haven soon were busy ports in the China trade. They brought in "Lowestoff" and other china coveted by prominent New England families. Brooks, p. 45 ff.; Harold D. Eberlein and Roger W. Ramsdell, *The Practical Book of Chinaware* (1925), p. 19.

Ebenezer Norton: J. W. Lewis, "Goshen of Ye Olden Days," in *History of Litchfield County* (1897), n.p. Information on the Norton family from William S. Norton, M.D., Washington, Connecticut, a direct descendant of Ebenezer.

Nathaniel Norton's New York State lands: Orsamus Turner, *The Phelps and Gorham Purchase and Morris Reserve* (1851).

Captain John Norton's pottery: John Spargo, *The Potters of Bennington* (1938), pp. 1–22; *Child's Bennington County Directory* (1800–1881), p. 87. In the captain's army career he stood at attention with the troops in New York to hear General

Washington read aloud a copy of the first issue of the Declaration of Independence. Later the captain was a guard at the hanging of the personable young English spy, Major John Andre indicted for complicity with Benedict Arnold in the plot to seize West Point for the British. Major Andre: Goulder, pp. 284, 285.

"Sketch of the History of the Hudson Family," presented by William Norton Hudson, in Hudson, Ohio in 1846.

Henry Hudson: Llewelyn Powys, *Henry Hudson* (1928).

In correspondence in 1936 by this writer with Powys and his collaborator Millard Hudson of Washington, D.C., both indicated they had had numerous inquiries about William Hudson's "genealogy." They had examined his statements thoroughly, they stated, and rejected them entirely. Millard Hudson (not related to the Ohio Hudsons) who, Powys declared, "knew more about Henry Hudson's family than any one ever had, or ever would know," wrote that in extensive research about the explorer's family he had carried on both in this country and in England, he had found only the three sons listed by Powys, and no son David.

Baldwin genealogy: compiled by Charles Candee Baldwin, printed in Cleveland, in 1881.

Reminiscences of Hudson, Ohio for One Hundred Years: published by the Hudson Independent, 1899.

DAVID HUDSON'S FIRST WESTERN ACRES

Epidemic land speculation: Merk, p. 116 ff.

Decision to sell the Reserve: Mary Lou Conlin, *Simon Perkins of the Reserve* (1968), p. 5 ff.

The Fire Lands and Salt Springs: William E. Peters, *Ohio Lands* (1930), p. 249; Hatcher, p. 52 ff.

Indian threats and sorties by Generals Harmar, St. Clair, and Wayne: Lodge, Vol. II, p. 92 ff.; Goulder, p. 247 ff.; Merk, p. 149.

The Treaty of Greenville: In signing this treaty the tribes relinquished two-thirds of the state of Ohio as well as part of Indiana and lands in the Illinois region. As a result, routes west became safe for travel by the white man. In turn the Indians were given $20,000 in treaty goods, with certain tribes receiving annuities of $9,500, others $1,000, and some $500. Merk, p. 150 ff.

The senior Hudson's will, filed June 7, 1794, probated April 13, 1799: Copies of both documents from Probate Records, Litchfield County Court House, Litchfield, Connecticut.

John Jay's treaty: Merk, pp. 151–52.

The Connecticut School fund: Information supplied by Samuel M. Fraulino, Special Funds Officer, Office of the Treasurer, State of Connecticut, and by Eunice Gillman Dibella, Assistant Archivist, Connecticut State Library. The fund continues today. The principal has more than doubled since the sale of the Western Reserve: in 1980 it amounted to about $2.8 million and has earned over $17 million since its inception. All of it has been used for educational purposes as required by the state constitution. These monies are invested in bonds, mutual funds, short term investments, and the like. Earnings for 1979–80 were $188,630. Such returns are transferred annually to the Connecticut General Fund from which appropriations are made to the State Department of Education. Little did land company officials realize that income from their western wilderness would help underwrite Connecticut schools for nearly two hundred years.

The sale took place in Hartford, August 5, 1795: Conlin, p. 6.

Ephraim Starr: Among Goshen stories about Starr's business deals, one describes his trips by ox cart to New York. It was at the end of the war. Tories assembled there in haste to leave the country and, needing cash, sold him their household goods for whatever he would pay. Draying his purchases back to Goshen, he disposed of them there and in neighboring communities at a good profit. Hibbard, p. 538.

Connecticut Land Company: Claude L. Shepard, *The Connecticut Land Company*, WRHS, 1916, Tract 96; Conlin, p. 8; Charles Whittlesey, *Early History of Cleveland* (1867), contains much information on the Reserve and the land company; Charles Cook Bronson, *The Bronson Book*, p. 7 ff. This book is a collection of pioneers' records and personal papers pertaining to the Reserve and the land company. The original was handwritten by Bronson, early settler of Tallmadge, Ohio, for the Summit and Portage County Pioneer Association. The present volume was edited and reproduced by the Stow Ohio Public Library, n.d. Copies in the Hudson Library and Historical Society (hereafter referred to as HLHS).

Early land purchases by Ephraim Kirby and Elijah Wadsworth, September 5, 1795 and purchase of 3,000 acres by David Hudson, October 10, 1795: deeds in Vol. 28, p. 25, The Recorder's Office, Summit County Court House, Akron, Ohio.

Hudson's Medina County land: Eleanor Iler Shapiro, *Wadsworth Heritage* (1964), p. 16 ff.

THE LAND COMPANY LEARNS ABOUT ITS PURCHASE

As a consequence of the eighteenth-century proclivity for journal-keeping, and the training in Connecticut public schools, the two early odysseys into the Western Reserve have been recorded in almost day-by-day detail by men who were able to transcribe their experiences in readable English. As a result, much information on these surveys has come down to present-day citizens of the Reserve. The Western Reserve Historical Society, Cleveland, has what must be one of the best collections on the subject, including daily journals and made-on-the-spot maps, some of the original documents. General Cleaveland's journal is reproduced as Tract 94. Other sources consulted for this chapter include: *The Bronson Book*, pp. 9–17; Whittlesey, pp. 162, 171–80, 184; Hatcher, p. 22 ff.; Karl H. Grismer, *Akron and Summit County*, n.d., p. 33 ff.; Randall and Ryan, pp. 580–87; and Bond, p. 362 ff.

Morse's Geography: This was the work of Jedidiah Morse, a Connecticut clergyman. It was the first geography published in the United States. He was the father of Samuel F. B. Morse, the portrait painter who invented the telegraph and experimented with cable telegraphy.

THE GREAT REAL ESTATE LOTTERY

Much of this chapter is based on the rich material at WRHS on the Connecticut Land Company and its purchase of the Western Reserve.

Purchasers and amount of original investment in the drawing of Hudson Township January 1798 in Book of Draughts, p. 9, WRHS repository:

Samuel Fowler	$1,546.77
Daniel Goodman and Timothy Allen	1,931.00
Ephraim Starr	6,000.00
Joseph Lyman	200.00
Julianna Hubbard	200.00
Enoch W. Thayer	1,200.00
David Hudson	900.00
Birdsey Norton and Elihu Lewis	300.00
Stephen W. Jones	.03
Roger Newberry, Justin Ely, Elijah White, and Jonathan Buss	625.43
Total	$12,903.23

Amount each land company member invested: *The Bronson Book*, pp. 7, 8.

Equalizing sections: "Some less desirable townships were set aside as 'equalizing' areas—a cumbersome method of partition but there is no record of difficulties that resulted." Shepard, WRHS Tract 96.

David Hudson's Geauga County property: In 1801 Hudson sold "Nathaniel Norton et al" 2,960 acres, price not indicated. General Index to Deeds, Geauga County, Vol. I, p. 271. The six and a quarter acres deeded to Geauga County by David Hudson for a park, Geauga County Records, Book 6, p. 213.

Purchase of one-eighth part of township by Parmele, Oviatt, and Baldwin: Vol. AA, pp. 5–6, Recorder's Office, Summit County Court House, Akron.

Through a loan by Birdsey and Nathaniel Norton, Hudson was able to acquire one-fourth interest in the township. Vol. AA, pp. 4–5, Recorder's Office, Summit County Court House, Akron.

Claim that the township was purchased for $8,320 with a 10,000 acre equalizing
grant: Anna Lee, great-great-granddaughter of David Hudson. "Period of
Settlement," p. 6, in a pamphlet, *A Short History of Hudson, Ohio*, reprint of
1950 edition, HLHS.

THE HOWLING WILDERNESS

Quitclaim agreements by Sarah Hudson: Copies obtained from the Litchfield County
Court House.

David Hudson's account of his re-conversion: This is in an article he wrote for the
Western Repository of Religious Intelligence, published in 1803. In this he also
declared he had been upset in boyhood by his father leaving the Congregational
church to join first the Baptists and then, even worse, the Quakers. However,
the elder Hudson had been appointed to the important local Committee of
Correspondence and he also served on local school boards. And after the
Revolutionary War he was listed as a patriot, recognition of non-military service
in the war effort. Goshen Town Hall Records, transcribed by Lewis M. Norton,
Vol. I., 1840, and Hibbard, p. 117. It is difficult to reconcile such apostasy at
a time when only men in good standing in the Congregational church were
eligible for public office. Could it have been only a temporary fall from
orthodoxy?

The map on page 48 of David Hudson's route from the Cuyahoga to his township
is based on the map and study by Waldo L. Semon in the HLHS.

The French Revolution: "The importance of the French Revolution on religious
thought [in Connecticut] cannot be over-emphasized. This was true until the
start of the blood-letting when Americans turned from the French," Richard
J. Purcell, *Connecticut in Transit* (1961), p. 2 ff.

The trip to the Ohio country: This is from Hudson's journal in which he recorded
day-by-day events. Copy in HLHS.

Nathaniel Norton in East Bloomfield: Coming via the route later followed by David
Hudson and all west-going pioneers, Norton arrived with his family and
numerous Norton relatives when the area was first opened to settlement. Fine
fields of corn and orchards planted by the Indians flourished in the rich, flat
land between stands of dense forest. Deer bounded through the openings,
wolves and bears prowled around the settlers' high-fenced pens of sheep, and
salmon swam up the river outlets. Norton prospered, became a community
leader, was appointed sheriff, and elected to the legislature. Turner, *Phelps
and Gorham Purchase*, pp. 2 ff., 187, 191; Charles F. Millikin, *History of Ontario
Country* (1911), pp. 206, 207; Correspondence with William S. Norton, M.D.,
Washington, Connecticut.

Lorenzo Carter: There are many references in the annals of early Cleveland to this
colorful first permanent settler. His cabin at the mouth of the Cuyahoga did
duty as home and tavern, schoolroom for settlers' children, setting for the first

"ball," headquarters for his lucrative trade with the Indians and his shipbuilding operations. Like Hudson and his party, all lake-borne incoming settlers were greated by Carter. In 1938 the Early Settlers Association dedicated a statue to Carter in Erie Street Cemetery. William Ganson Rose, *Cleveland, the Making of a City* (1950), pp. 35, 38, 45, 46 ff., 947.

HUDSON'S FIRST SETTLERS ARRIVE

The drawing on page 50, entitled "Landing of the Surveyors," is from *Pioneers of the Western Reserve* by Harvey Rice.

David Hudson's second trip west: Extensive information in his journals and in his papers, HLHS; *The Bronson Book*, p. 67 ff.; William Henry Perrin, *History of Summit County* (1881), p. 411 ff.

Nathaniel Norton: His 325 acres, originally part of the large Phelps-Gorham tract, was in a beautiful part of New York State west of the Finger Lakes in Ontario County. In the early histories much was written about this section and the boat building indigenous to the area. Norton's mills, his trading post, distillery, and similar pioneer industries were well paying. He made money also in land speculation endemic to the region. He managed to have some of the profitable local boat building also carried on on his farm. Orsamus Turner, *History of Pioneer Settlements* (1861), and Turner, *Phelps and Gorham Purchase;* Lewis Cass Aldrich, *History of Ontario County* (1861); Whittlesey. Additional information from R. Donald Muller, Director, Ontario Historical Society, Canandaigua, New York, and from Marion Thomas, Gorham Historical Society, Gorham, New York. Additional Norton family data from William S. Norton, M.D., Washington, Connecticut.

The Quieting Act: Shepard, p. 61 ff.; David Lindsey, *Ohio's Western Reserve: The Story of its Place Names* (1955), pp. 1–4, 13, 101; Goulder, pp. 40, 41.

The montage of views of the David Hudson house and farm (on page 57) was prepared by Hudson artist Horace Rogers and presented to Anner Hudson Baldwin on her ninetieth birthday.

. . . AND A NEW TOWN CAME INTO BEING

The drawing on page 58 is from *Squirrel Hunters of Ohio* by Nelson Edwards Jones.

This chapter is based to a large extent on David Hudson's journal entries.

Westward movement of people: Frederick Jackson Turner, "The Significance of Frontier History," in *The Annals of America* (1884–94), Vol. II, p. 462 ff. Newspapers in Connecticut broke out with a rash of advertisements and news stories about the opportunities in the west, playing down Indian attacks. The Ohio fever continued and the Yankees migrated. Holbrook, pp. 35, 108 ff.

Hudson family records, kindly made available by Mrs. Eber Hyde of Claridon, Ohio, a direct descendant of David Hudson.

The Oviatt family history is from the privately printed *History of the Newton and Oviatt Families* (1875), pp. 20–32.

The drawing of Indians spearing fish on page 61 and the woodcut entitled "Pennsylvania" on page 64 are courtesy of the Western Reserve Historical Society. The drawing of the Connecticut State Seal on page 66 is by John Warner Barber, from *Connecticut Historical Collections*, 1836. The photogravure of the Charter Oak on page 67 is after the painting by C. D. W. Brownell circa 1855 and is courtesy of the Connecticut Historical Society.

SALVATION IN A SADDLEBAG

Organization of Hudson Township: Samuel A. Lane, *Akron and Summit County* (1891), p. 817.

David Hudson's trip to Goshen: based on his journals in HLHS archives.

Purchase of books in Goshen: Hudson's journal, HLHS archives.

The coming of the Reverend Joseph Badger: Badger's *Memoir*, published by Sawyer, Ingersoll and Company, Hudson, Ohio, 1851.

Tenets of Calvinistic theology: Milton Rugoff, *The Beechers* (1981), p. 8 ff., and in numerous references to the Reverend Lyman Beecher, eloquent protagonist of the creed.

Transfer of former members of the Goshen Congregational Church to the church in Hudson: "Goshen Congregational Church on August 30, 1801 voted a certificate of regular standing" to the eleven named, Goshen Congregational Church Records, 1801.

Sesquicentennial of Hudson's first church: Raymond A. Mickel, "Historical Markers of Hudson," (1964), a pamphlet.

THE BACONS

David Bacon and family in Hudson, and contemporary events: The David Hudson collection, HLHS.

Tallmadge was drawn in Draft 24 as Township 2, Range 10. It was divided roughly into three sections: 6,105 acres purchased by Brace and Associates for $6,105; 5,611 acres by Tallmadge for $4,800; and the third, 3,493 acres by Starr for $2,935. The township was surveyed in 1803 by General Simon Perkins of Warren. Bacon had what he acquired also surveyed and moved his family to the township in 1807. *The Bronson Book*, pp. 18 ff., 27 ff.

Tallmadge, including David Bacon's plans for a church-dominated community: Lane, pp. 1032–59; Perrin, p. 552 ff.; Henry Howe, *Historical Collections of Ohio* (1904), Vol. II, pp. 640–45.

All her life Delia won the support of influential individuals. Before she left for
England, Ralph Waldo Emerson, although repudiating her Shakespeare theme,
wrote letters of introduction for her to Carlyle, Hawthorne, and other
prominent English friends. They, also rejecting her idea, nonetheless welcomed
her warmly. Carlyle and his wife enjoyed her visits and wanted her to live
with them. "Take the back room," Carlyle had said, "It's always empty." But
instead she went to Stratford-upon-Avon, where Shakespeare is buried in Holy
Trinity Church. She had hoped to open the grave, certain that records in it
would confirm her ideas about the plays. But the vicar refused her permission.
She became a frequent visitor to the site. Coming at night with her lantern
bobbing in the darkness like a firefly, she moved up front to sit quietly near
the grave. The vicar gave instructions that she was not to be disturbed, and
an attendant stood quietly at the rear until she departed. Vivian C. Hopkins,
Prodigal Puritan, Life of Delia Bacon (1959). In this excellent study, the author
presents also colorful details about David Bacon, his missionary labors before
coming to Ohio, and much about his Tallmadge project.

A pamphlet, "Proceedings of the Fiftieth Anniversary of the Settlement of
Tallmadge," contains the speech by Leonard Bacon, his reminiscences of his
arrival with his family from Hudson, other addresses, and the history of the
town to date.

The illustration on pages 86–87 of the Tallmadge Center Park is from the *Historical
Atlas of Summit County, Ohio, 1874.*

JOHN BROWN COMES TO HUDSON

In 1921 the Reverend Clarence S. Gee, pastor of Hudson's Congregational church,
discovered in going over church records that John Brown as a youth had joined
the church, then in the log structure on the green. Further search revealed
that he and Dianthe Lusk, also a member, were married in the new church in
1820, probably shortly after it was built on the site of the present Town Hall
at East Main and Church streets. He found that there were a few older
residents in Hudson who remembered John Brown, and many more who had
grown up with tales of the controversial personality handed down by their
parents. He called on these people, took notes on what they told him, and
soon was launched in what eventually would become a lifetime interest.

Gee left Hudson for other posts. But he never forgot his initiation into the
John Brown lore. When he retired and was living in Lockport, New York, he
resumed his quest, and with increasing enthusiasm gave the rest of his life to
it. He soon was in touch with another John Brown enthusiast, Boyd B. Stutler
of Charleston, West Virginia where Brown had been imprisoned and executed
(then it was Charles Town, Virginia).

The two men, conferring frequently with each other, had one overriding goal
in common, to locate the original autobiographical letter John's father Owen

Brown had written in 1850. Excerpts had appeared in early books, brief and edited beyond anything the writer could have produced. It had been written at the request of his daughter Sally Marian who married Titus Hand at Grafton, Ohio and signed her letters Marian S.

Stutler had followed many false clues, and Gee likewise as he took up the search. Finally after many years of effort Gee found a Brown descendant, Mrs. Marian Clement who had the letter tucked away in her trailer in Yucaipa, California. She would not relinquish it, nor let it be taken out of California. Mrs. Gee joined her husband and copied the entire, lengthy document, meticulously preserving the difficult spelling. They made out all of it, but one word. The one disappointment for Gee was that Boyd Stutler had died before the discovery and could not share the triumph.

Two Hudson residents who knew Gee and Stutler, and had become interested in the John Brown story, in 1964 gave the Hudson Library and Historical Society microfilm copies of the Stutler manuscript collection, purchased from the Ohio State Historical Society.

A few years later Gee made known he intended to leave his collection to the Hudson Library and in 1970 the first section was received. Especially valuable sections making up a quarter of the whole and the heart of the collection arrived four years later. It included also important items gathered by Howard H. Clark of Kent, Ohio, grandson of Jeremiah Brown, John's half brother.

The Hudson Library and Historical Society now has one of the finest assemblages of data on John Brown to be found in the country. The librarian and curator, Thomas L. Vince, engrossed in the riches that had befallen his institution, was soon an authority himself on Hudson's one-time citizen. Interest in Brown, whether viewed as martyr or felon, goes unabated, and scholars come to the library from all parts of the country as far away as Hawaii.

Owen Brown's first home in Hudson was a log cabin he had built on his first trip in 1804. According to an early settler, it stood "where Grimm's store was," the northeast corner of the Cleveland Road and the Aurora-Hudson Road. Owen had sold his Torrington property and "had been somewhat prosperous," he stated in his autobiography. He soon was extending his acreage east along Aurora Road. Within a few months he was buying additional land in the village and township: ninety-seven and a quarter acres from David Hudson for a little over $1,000; two and a half acres of a mechanics lot from Stephen Thompson for $60; eight acres in the township from John Singleterry for $20. He continued buying and selling property, becoming a substantial landowner.

The pine tree at Ruth Brown's grave: Emily Metcalf in her account of the new church of 1820; copy in files of the Hudson Congregational Church.

John Brown's letter with reminiscences of his boyhood: It was written in 1857 to Henry Stearns, whose father, George Stearns, had helped him on several occasions, at one time contributing over two hundred dollars for land at North Elba. Young Stearns had asked Brown about his boyhood; copy in Gee collection, HLHS. Also found in F. B. Sanborn, *The Life and Letters of John Brown* (1891), pp. 12–17.

Sally Root: She was born in Massachusetts, the oldest child of the Jeremiah Roots. Her mother came from an intellectual family whose men for generations were Harvard graduates. Sally's sister Abigail married Dr. Jonathan Metcalf. Their daughter Emily organized a successful school for young women in Hudson, and was active in village affairs. In marrying Owen, Sally assumed the care of his four sons, his daughter Ruth, and Levi Blakeslee. Sally became the mother of eight children. She died of consumption in 1840.

Christian Cackler: "Recollections of an Old Settler," an undated pamphlet.

THE COMING OF THE ELLSWORTHS

Elisha's letter: From the scrapbook collection of items relating to early Hudson maintained by Grace Ellsworth Forbush, daughter of Elisha Martin Ellsworth. Elisha's letter, courtesy of Mrs. Forbush's daughter, Louise Forbush Boyd. Mrs. Forbush lived for many years in the house where she was born. It was on a 265-acre farm laid out by her father at the eastern end of Aurora Road, close to the Portage County line. The house erected in 1881 is similar to the earlier house built by her father's father, Augustus Ellsworth, on the Cleveland Road (Route 91) at the corner of Post's Lane.

Ellsworth family genealogy details: Lincoln Ellsworth, *James W. Ellsworth, His Life and Ancestry* (1930), Vols. I, II.

The drawing on pages 104–5 of William W. Ellsworth's residence on Ravenna Road is from the *Historical Atlas of Summit County, Ohio, 1874*. Note the college brick row on the hill in the background.

THE WAR OF 1812

News of "The second war with Great Britain" reaches Cleveland: Rose, p. 69.

The war and its effect on northern Ohio: William T. Utter, *After Tippecanoe: Some Aspects of the War of 1812* (1963), pp. 88 ff.

Owen Brown references to the war: autobiographical letter, Gee collection, HLHS.

John Brown's experiences in the War of 1812: from his letter to young Henry Stearns written in 1857; copy in Sanborn, pp. 12–17, and in Gee collection, HLHS.

Hudson citizens participate in the war: Hudson Annals, HLHS; *Ohio Registry War of 1812*, published by the Adjutant General of Ohio, 1915; Perrin, p. 429 ff.

The Chauncey Case family arrived in Hudson in 1814: Lora Case, *Hudson of Long Ago*, reminiscences originally published in *The Hudson Independent*, February–August 1897, edited and reprinted 1963 by HLHS through the generosity of four Hudson rsidents, Lora's great-grandsons Weldon W., Nelson H., Baxter H., and Theodore H. Case.

Early school curriculum: Shirley Glubok, ed., *Home and Child Life in Colonial Days* (1969); Cornelia Meigs, *A Critical History of Children's Literature* (1953).

A license for an inn and for dispensing liquor was issued several times to David
Hudson, the first probably in 1813: Hudson Annals, HLHS; Perrin, p. 433.

Anna Hudson's death and David Hudson's marriage to Mary Robinson: records in
HLHS. Few details are available about David Hudson's second wife. Her
portrait, however, was painted by James Beard in June 1829 as a companion
piece to the full-length study of Squire Hudson by the same artist at that time.
The second Mrs. Hudson, who had no children, died in 1847.

The Reverend William Hanford bought and sold considerable land, mostly along
Aurora Street west from the church lot. A house amidst a well-cared for lawn,
now 161 Aurora Street, stands where the parsonage cabin once was. The rest
of Hanford's farm along Aurora Street is also given to homes and gardens.

The drawing on page 112 of pioneers heading west is courtesy of the Western
Reserve Historical Society. Reproduced on page 115 is the last letter of John
Brown written to Lora Case on December 2, 1859. It is now in the Berg
Collection of the New York Public Library.

A FINE NEW CHURCH

The Congregational Church of 1820: This information is based on a paper, "History
of the Hudson Church," by Miss Emily Metcalf. It was read during the
centennial celebration in 1902 at the morning service. "First Congregational
Church, Hudson, Ohio," a pamphlet, (1902), p. 20.

The sketch of Dr. Moses Thompson on page 117 is from *Fifty Years and Over of
Akron* by Samuel A. Lane. The illustration on page 121 is an 1865 postcard
picturing the Congregational church.

DIANTHE

Long after John Brown had died, his house on Hines Hill by a queer quirk of fate
became the home of a widow, Mrs. Earl Johnson, who had been brought up
on tales about him. Her uncle, Richard Realf, like Mrs. Johnson a native of
England, was a poet and one of the idealistic young men whom Brown attracted.
Realf seems to have made several trips across the Atlantic, on one voyage
coming on a slave ship that he might learn firsthand about the treatment
endured by the manacled blacks.

Mrs. Johnson, then Minnie Alice Whapham, was only ten when Realf died.
She had seen a great deal of him, however, both in England and in America,
and remembered he always called her "Frisky." She treasured yellowed letters
in beautiful prose that she had received from him as well as faded photographs
and a biographical memoir. And she also had a little volume of his poetry put
together by his American companion-in-arms Richard J. Hinton, another of
Brown's disciples.

Realf, according to Mrs. Johnson, was started on his writing career by his mother, who had more than the usual education for English girls of that day. Neighboring "gentry" attracted by the youth's charm and intellect welcomed him in their homes. When he was seventeen two events greatly influenced his life: he brought out his first book of poetry which gained recognition from Lady Byron, and he read *Uncle Tom's Cabin*, thereby developing a zealous concern for the American slave.

When Realf arrived in America a few years later, John Brown was traveling here and there and everywhere "in the name of God and the black man." Realf followed him to Kansas, an experience that inspired his poem "Defense of Lawrence," and other verses dedicated to abolition. He lectured extensively to raise money for the cause, speaking before gatherings in Akron, Warren, and Cleveland, his distinguished appearance and eloquent oratory making him a popular platform figure.

In the Civil War, Realf joined an Illinois regiment, promptly being promoted to colonel. All the while he managed to write his verses that were to win him recognition as "the unfamed Shelley of America." But marital troubles, broken health, and poor pay for his writing so discouraged him that he took his life in 1878.

The drawing on page 128 of a cabin in the woods is by Henry Howe, from *Historical Collections of Ohio*. The illustration on page 129 is of the headstones marking the gravesite of Dianthe and her baby Frederick on the former John Brown farm in New Richmond, Pennsylvania.

MARY ANNE

Much about the tragic Richfield years was supplied by Mrs. W. R. Simpson of Kent, granddaughter of Edward Brown, half brother of John; also by Mrs. Dorothy Sykes, librarian, Richfield Public Library; and by Miss Jennie Oviatt, whose grandmother helped Mary during this time.

The drawing of Colonel Simon Perkins is from *Fifty Years and Over of Akron* by Samuel A. Lane.

The North Elba home: Edwin N. Cotter, Jr., superintendent of the John Brown farm at North Elba and an authority on John Brown and his family, contributed many details about their life at the northern outpost.

F. B. Sanborn, *The Life and Letters of John Brown* (1891); Richard O. Boyer, *The Legend of John Brown* (1973).

WESTERN RESERVE COLLEGE

Frederick Clayton Waite, *Western Reserve University, the Hudson Era* (1943), pp. 1–89. Dr. Waite was born in Hudson "on the edge of the campus." Both his grandfathers contributed to the college when it was founded, and his father worked on the first college buildings. He was graduated from Western Reserve College after it moved to Cleveland and for many years was a professor at Western Reserve University.

C. H. Cramer, *Case Western Reserve, a History of the University, 1826–1976* (1976), pp. 3–20. Dr. Cramer was a professor at Western Reserve University and also when it became Case Western Reserve University.

Helen H. Kitzmiller, *One Hundred Years of Western Reserve* (1926), published as part of the centennial of the founding of Western Reserve Academy, at Hudson, 1926, pp. 9–30. The little book presents a vivid picture of the austere campus life in the beginning days.

Information from early documents and records of the college kindly supplied by Archivist Ruth W. Helmuth of Case Western Reserve University.

Information on Lemuel Porter of Waterbury from the Mattatuck Museum, Waterbury, Connecticut.

Birdsey Norton Oviatt post office theft: Annals of Cleveland, 1818–1935, Vol. III, Abstract 103, February 1821, Abstract 105, March 20, 1821, WRHS. According to a record in the Portage County Historical Society files, a bond of $300 was posted in 1826 for the care of Mary (or Mercy) Oviatt, orphan daughter of Birdsey Norton Oviatt. The bond was signed by Heman Oviatt (Birdsey's father), Harvey Baldwin, and David Hudson. Nothing more has come to light about the child or her future.

David Hudson's letter concerning his dismissal as postmaster: Hudson citizens were indignant at this treatment of the squire and a reprint of his long letter appeared September 1, 1829 in the *Western Intelligencer*, at that time published in the village. Writing in high dudgeon Hudson described his "sacrifices for his country during the War." He and his brother, who obviously had been drafted, "had, with a large sum of money hired a good soldier to enlist during the War. . . . Repeatedly my house was stripped of every rag of clothes to supply the naked soldier who was fighting our battles. . . . I have gratuitously cut the grain for the women whose fathers, husbands and brothers were in the 'tented field.'" He had "sacrificed a large share of my property in affecting our Independence." He added a final plea: "Should you, Sir, continue me in office for a few days until Death shall save you the trouble of ejecting me I trust I shall continue the faithful discharge of the duties that short time."

Hiring a substitute seems to have roused little approbrium in New England in the Revolutionary War. At a Goshen Town Meeting in 1780 it was voted to pay whoever served for six months the sum of forty shillings bounty money whether he volunteered or was drafted. And "any person being drafted who shall hire another to take his place . . . is to receive the bounty."

In 1833 Colonel Porter's widow, Margaret Porter, bought a house—since then much changed—at 48 Aurora Street and lived there many years, making a home for her seven children.

South and Middle Colleges have been razed, but the double house known as the President's House still is in use. It has been described as "the most handsome of all the campus buildings. . . . The delicate proportions give the house a certain distinction equal to any New England counterpart."

THE FIRST COLLEGE PRESIDENTS

Data from Ruth Helmuth, archivist, Case Western Reserve University; Cramer; and Waite.
Student life in the early days from Kitzmiller.
Diary of John Buss, HLHS.
The building pictured on page 160 is correctly called the Free Congregational Church, but it was usually referred to as the Oberlin Church because its preachers came from Oberlin College. The original church occupied the top two stories of the building in this photo.
The illustration on page 162 is an old drawing of Western Reserve College by W. T. Norman, engraved in Hudson.

DAVID HUDSON JUNIOR AND THE NEW DOCTOR

David Hudson junior: The references to him are from his journal in which he recorded his daily activities from 1825 to 1836. The original manuscript is in the Western Reserve Historical Society.
Dr. Israel Town and wife: The Towns were given to letter writing. The extensive collection of these letters in HLHS is the basis for much of the data about the Towns. I am indebted also to Lois Newkirk who shared with me research on the Towns.
The Israel Town house, pictured on page 171, was built in 1831 in high Greek Revival style and elaborately remodeled in 1881 in Victorian style by the Neibel family. It is now the Johnson-Romito Funeral Home.
The Van Renesselaer Humphrey house at 264 North Main Street (see illustration page 172) was built in the early 1830s and extensively remodeled during the Victorian period.
The old woodcut of a horse and buggy on page 173 is from the transportation collection at the Western Reserve Historical Society.

THE BREWSTERS

The illustration on page 175 is an early advertising flyer used by Anson A. Brewster.
The Brewster family's personal papers were given to the HLHS in 1974 by the late Dorothy Parsons, a direct descendant of Anson A. Brewster, Jr. Miss

Parsons also gave the library many artifacts and portraits of the Brewsters, including oil portraits of Anson Jr. and Sarah Porter White Brewster.

The diaries of John Buss (written 1833–74) are in the collections of the HLHS. In 1942, Frederick C. Waite made an abstract of the diaries' contents as well as a complete transcription for the years 1833–36.

The 1861 photograph on page 182 shows *from left to right:* the Brewster store and Brewster store extension, the Brewster Mansion, Christ Church Episcopal, the Isham-Beebe house, and the Methodist church.

HUDSON DIES, COLLEGE EXPANDS, VILLAGE INCORPORATES

The portraits of Anner and Harvey Baldwin on pages 186–87 are by J. O. Osborne circa 1850 and are owned by descendant Virginia Bartholomew Hyde.

The drawings on pages 190 and 192 of the David Hudson house are by Horace Rogers, 1890.

The photograph on page 193 of Anner Maria Hudson Baldwin, taken on the occasion of her ninetieth birthday, shows *clockwise from upper right:* Harriet Gregory Whiting (Mrs. Julius Whiting), with Helen Anna Whiting in buggy; Edwin Lee; Marjorie Lee; Anna Gregory Lee (Mrs. Henry Lee), holding Anna V. Lee; Clarissa Baldwin Gregory; and, in the center, Anner Maria.

Although the Loomis Observatory, pictured on page 197, is the third oldest observatory in the country, it is the oldest still standing on its original foundation.

A NEW ELLSWORTH BABY AND HUDSON'S RAILROAD ERA

The illustration on page 199 is of the Pentagon and the cheese factory, with the Congregational church in the background. The Pentagon was demolished in 1909. In 1910 James Ellsworth remodeled the Straight and Company cheese warehouse into the Hudson Club House. It is now Hayden Hall.

Ellsworth references: Lincoln Ellsworth, Vols. I and II.

Henry N. Day: William Miller, *H. N. Day: A Study in Good Works* (1952); Waite, p. 182. I am indebted to Thomas L. Vince, librarian and curator, HLHS for use of his extensive notes from an address on Day's Hudson activities.

Early Hudson architect-builders: Research by Priscilla Graham; information on Lemuel Porter from the Silas Bronson Library, Waterbury, Connecticut.

Proof of Starr as builder of Birge Ellsworth's store: a bill for "work on store" signed by "E. B. Ellsworth and L. Starr," unpublished senior paper by Timothy Wittman, Hiram College, 1979.

The three Hudson Clinton line railroads: The Clinton line, 1852; the Clinton line extension, 1853; and the Hudson-Painesville line, 1853.

THE RETURN

The illustration on page 210 has been attributed to Hudson artist Horace Rogers.

Ellsworth references: Lincoln Ellsworth, *James W. Ellsworth;* Lincoln Ellsworth, *Beyond Horizons* (1937); J. F. Waring, *James W. Ellsworth and the Refounding of Western Reserve Academy* (1961); interview with Ada Cooper Miller, daughter of Harry Cooper, a miner later in charge of the grounds and gardens at Evamere.

The photographs on pages 212 and 213 show the Aurora-Main Street corner as it appeared before the improvements instituted by James Ellsworth. The illustrations on pages 215 and 216 are of James Ellsworth's estate, Evamere. The illustration on page 217 shows Western Reserve College as it appeared shortly after South College was demolished in 1884. James Ellsworth replaced South and Middle Colleges in 1914 with Seymour Hall.

The illustration on page 218 of the Hudson Union School, which was built in 1868 on Oviatt Street, is from the postcard collection of Judy Bee. The postcard illustration on page 219 is of the Aurora Street thoroughfare to James Ellsworth's house.

The picture on page 220 of James Ellsworth is from a family album now in the Western Reserve Academy archives.

The illustration on page 223 of the Western Reserve Academy chapel grown up to weeds is from Judy Bee's postcard collection.

The drawing "Looking East towards Hudson" on page 225 is by Betsy Guldan.

EPILOGUE

The illustration on page 229 shows Main Street shortly after 1912 when the clock tower was built.

The train pictured on page 230 is pulling in to Hudson's Peninsula Road or Streetsboro Street depot.

The pen and ink drawing of Anna Lee is by Hudson artist Avis Andres.

Louella Crawford Dodds, 1879–1978, pictured on page 238, was a longtime friend and traveling companion to James Ellsworth and his wife and a longtime trustee of the Hudson Library and Historical Society.

Turner's Mill is pictured on page 245. The Buss store, shown on page 246, burned in 1892.

The illustration on page 248 is a 1923 photo of Everett Shumate's gasoline station. The Western Reserve Telephone Company parking lot now occupies this site. The photo on page 249 is the view across the street of Main and Clinton streets.

John Morse kindly supplied the photograph on page 251 of himself and his cousin.

INDEX